From the Collection of...

Lisa Baldwin

To Alan, John, Joel, and Rebecca
and to all the wise ones who learn the stories and share them.
—JTE

To Sylvia,
Orville, Jr., Christie, and Jenny Lynn,
Wayne, Donnie, Curt, and Joe
—OH

My Old Mountain Home

I'd like to go back to my childhood days—
No car, no TV, no telephones.
Just a simple way of living
In my good old mountain home.

I'd like to walk once more out the old road.
Smell Mama's cornbread cooking on the old wood stove.
And when I get to the gate, I still can hear Mama holler,
"Better get to the house, young'uns. It's getting late."

There stands the old woodshed and the apple trees
And the haystacks I once played on.
Oh, what a beautiful sight,
My old mountain home.

There stands the old house,
Mama out in the yard.
Why, there comes Daddy out from the fields
Where he had been working hard.

When the day's work was over and done,
Me, Mary, and Jerry still had some time for fun.
Mama would holler, "Come set on the porch and rest a spell."
And there before bed time she would tell us a tale.

I know those days are past and gone.
But I will always have a sweet memory
Of my mountain home.

Today I live a little different kind of life,
For with five boys and a wife,
We have a car, a TV, and a telephone
In our little old mountain home.

I'd like to thank a friend of mine
For taking me back home one more time.
For this book about my childhood ways
Is the closest I'll get back to the good old days.

— Orville Hicks, 2005

Contents

Orville Hicks at the Jack Tales Festival, 2003

Preface

I first spoke with Orville Hicks in January of 2003. While working on a project about root and herb gathering, I had found his name in a master's thesis at Appalachian State University. The thesis identified Orville as one who had gathered herbs, so I looked up his telephone number and called him. We talked for forty-five minutes. I was surprised that he shared his time with me so willingly.

Orville spoke of learning stories from his mother as they gathered galax. He heard her stories in the evening as they sat on the porch and tied the day's galax harvest into bunches. These glimpses of his personal story stirred my interest.

Orville and I are about the same age and are both native North Carolinians, but our childhood worlds were far apart in many ways. Yet he spoke of a world that had touched my own and fascinated me for many years—the mountains, native plants, gardening, an uncluttered lifestyle, stories.

In June I drove two hours to the Todd General Store to hear Orville tell tales. I was intrigued by his storytelling. Who was this man who told old stories and couldn't contain his own laughter at them? His laughter was genuine, not proud.

Soon afterward, I knew what I had to do. I had to write a picture book for children about how Orville learned stories from his mother. I called him and proposed the idea. "That'd be all right," he said.

In September I met with Orville and his wife, Sylvia, at their home in Deep Gap, North Carolina. We talked for four hours. I took pages of notes. I had already written a rough draft of my idea. Orville liked it. The only problem was that my plan was too narrow. He had so much more to share.

So we decided on a longer book.

Over the months that followed, I met with Orville many times—at his home, at story-telling events, on the mountain where he grew up. Every time, I left in awe of Orville, who lives with one foot in the present and one in the past.

Who is this storyteller with overflowing laughter? Hear his own story as he offered it to me.

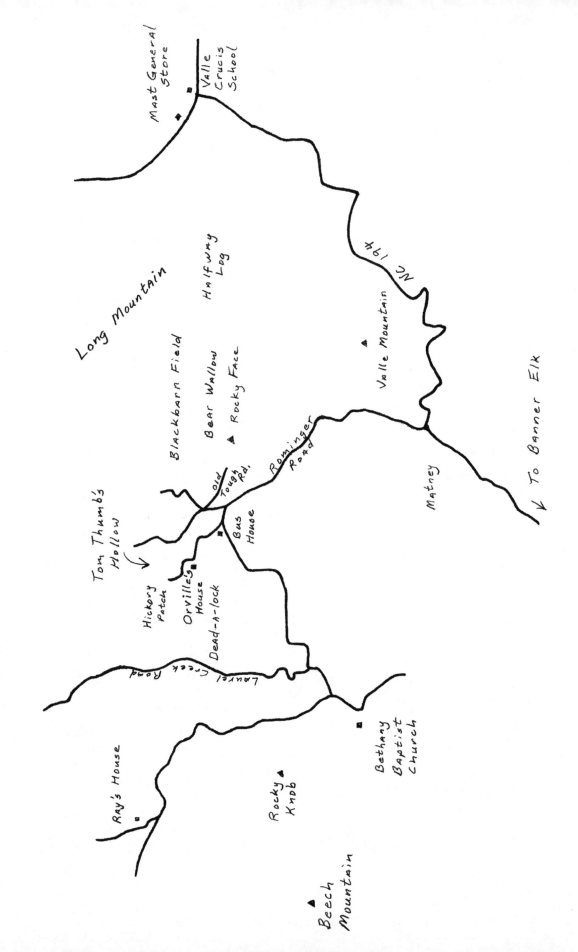

PART I.

The Storyteller and His Time

Orville Hicks is the best of the current Jack Tale tellers.
—Thomas McGowan, folklorist, Appalachian State University

A tall, sturdy man dressed in overalls and sporting a full beard takes a seat before the crowd. The cap he wears reads, "Hicks Tree Service." His eyes sparkle as he speaks.

Well, howdy, everybody. My name's Orville Hicks, and I was raised up on the back side of Beech Mountain, North Carolina.

Listen as Orville Hicks tells his tales—Jack Tales, other traditional tales, and slices of life from the North Carolina mountains. As you listen, expect to hear laughter. Some will likely be your own. Some will be Orville's, deep-voiced and bubbling from the heart. His laughter reveals a comfort with life, past and present. It reveals a love of his heritage and a love of the lore.

In 1951, when Orville was born, electricity had been lighting homes for decades. It offered the convenience of toasters, hair dryers, washing machines, and even televisions. Telephones and cars brought people together despite distance.

But this image did not fit all of America. Change bypassed numerous pockets of the country. Beech Mountain, North Carolina, and the hills and hollows surrounding it were among those places where change came slowly. This was the world in which Orville Hicks grew up.

Folks in the mountain community worked hard yet still had time to talk, visit, and swap tales. High in a mountain hollow, a mother told stories to her children as they worked together in the garden and as they gathered herbs in the woods. Orville Hicks heard his mother's stories again and again until he learned

Looking toward Orville's home
from Beech Mountain.
Rocky Face rises above the other peaks.

them by heart. Later, as he roamed the woods alone, he remembered his mother's tales. In time, woods and words came together in the stories of Orville Hicks.

For over two hundred years, Orville's ancestors had settled on Beech Mountain and in nearby areas. Storytelling took root in these hills and hollows through at least six generations. The voices of storytellers have eased work, warmed cold nights, and strengthened family ties.

Orville Hicks follows the storytelling tradition of his family. Cousin and mentor Ray Hicks (1922–2003) was widely known for the folktales he told and for his mountain ways and speech. The Smithsonian Institution deemed him a national treasure. Ray recognized Orville as the torchbearer, the one who would continue to share the tales beyond the community.

The stories Orville tells include Jack Tales and other traditional tales. The well-known "Jack and the Beanstalk" is but one of many tales about Jack. This poor boy often scrounges to find a way to support himself and his mother. Tricksters, including his brothers Tom and Will, try to take advantage of Jack, but he cleverly escapes their schemes. Beech Mountain storytellers have swapped Jack Tales, including "Jack and the Varmints," "Jack and the Heifer Hide," and "Big Jack and Little Jack."

Folktales, such as "Catskin," "Gallymander," and "Soap, Soap, Soap," feature other characters and have been called "Jack Tales for girls."

Orville tells his tales in the colorful language of the Beech Mountain region. "Brothers" are "bruvers." "Climbed" is "cloom." "You" is "you'uns." A sack is a "poke." Chicks are called "diddles," and "boomers" are little red squirrels that skitter through the woods. A fellow with a "hog dollar" has a silver dollar, which was enough to buy a hog years ago. Orville's language is a rich inheritance from pioneering ancestors who came to Beech Mountain from Germany, England, and Scotland.

Orville tells a story of his uncles and their horses:

Well, I had two uncles back in the mountains there. They went out 'n bought 'em a horse apiece. When they got the horses home, got to lookin' at 'em, one of them said, "How we gonna tell these horses apart?"

Then one said, "Let's measure 'em, see which one's the longest."

They got their ruler out and measured the horses 'n both of 'em was the same longness. They measured 'em this other way and both of 'em was the same tallness, an' they still couldn't tell 'em apart.

One uncle said, "What we gonna do?"

The other uncle said, "I know what I'll do. I'll take the scissors, cut a piece out o' my horse's ear." He got the scissors, cut a little piece out of his horse's ear. He said, "Now we can tell 'em apart."

Well, that night the other horse got hung in a barbed wire fence 'n tore a piece of its ear off.

They went there the next mornin' to get 'em, and they couldn't tell 'em apart. So one uncle said, "What're we gonna do now? How're we gonna tell 'em apart?"

Then the other uncle said, "I'll clip part of mine's tail off." He cut three or four inches of his horse's tail off.

But that night the other horse got hung in a barbed wire fence, pulled part o' its tail off.

They got down there lookin' at 'em, an' one said, "What are we gonna do now? How're we gonna tell 'em apart?"

That other one said, "'Bout the only thing I know to do, you keep the black one, let me keep the white one."

Orville tells stories at the Moses Cone Manor on the Blue Ridge Parkway, 2004.

Orville, the
eleventh child

Hattie and Hassell,
the first two children

PART II.

Childhood

FAMILY

We was just one big family.
We all stuck together—we worked together, played together.
When one hit the field, we all hit the field.
—Orville

In May of 1951, new beadwood leaves budded from bare branches, and the first pink lady slippers opened. Orville Gold Hicks was born on May 6 that year. He was "the baby one," the eleventh child of Gold and Sarah Harmon Hicks, yet he bore his father's name.

"Only the last three of us were born in a hospital," Orville says.

Home was "on the back side of the Beech," as Orville says, in the Rominger community near Matney and Valle Mountain. Orville's parents both had long family histories in the Beech Mountain region. Many kinfolk lived nearby. As Orville grew up, he and his family walked the wooded paths across the mountain as often as they traveled the winding dirt roads that led around them.

Orville had six brothers and four sisters. By the time Orville was born, some older siblings had married and moved on. Mary and Jerry, the twins, remained at home, as did Willis. Nancy married while Orville was young, and Bobby died while Orville was still a child.

Orville (top left) with his nephews: Paul, Bobby, Ronald, and Sylvester Hicks

Orville, Mary and Jerry (in back) with Charlie's children, Bobby and Brenda, 1962

Orville's oldest brother, Hassell, lived on the mountain as well. Hattie, John, and Charlie moved to other towns, but they later heeded the call of their roots and returned to the mountain community. Only Frances and Nancy remained beyond Watauga County.

For Orville, life centered on family. Playmates, work companions, and role models came from family, and family introduced Orville to stories.

Mary and Jerry

Mama: Sarah Harmon Hicks, Heiress of Stories (1908-1986)

Most of my tales I learned from listening to Mama.
She was a great storyteller.
—Orville

Sarah Hicks offered her children the gifts of love and legacy. Her children respected her and listened to her.

"Mama was always real nice, always smiling," says Orville. "You had to work hard to make her mad, but if you made her mad, she was mad!"

Cornbread was a staple on the Hickses' table. "Mama'd bake a big old cake of cornbread and set it on the stove during the day. She'd tell us young'uns, 'You get hungry, there's some cornbread on the stove.'" Orville relished sneaking back to the kitchen to get cornbread—not that sneaking was necessary after Mama's invitation. "I'd reach up and grab a chunk to eat."

Mama also nourished her family with stories. She had learned the stories from her father and grandfather and from her older brothers, but her storytelling roots ran deeper yet.

Cutliff Harman, or Harmon (1748-1838), Mama's great-great-grandfather, came through the mountains with frontiersman Daniel Boone. Boone had hired Cutliff Harman to deliver goods from Yadkin Valley, North Carolina, to Tennessee. The land in what is now Watauga County was so pretty that Cutliff bought 522 acres and brought his wife and six children to settle there. While Cutliff built a house, his family camped under an overhanging rock in what is now Cove Creek.

The origin of mountain Jack Tales and other traditional tales is a mystery. Cutliff or his neighbor Samuel Hix, later Hicks, in Valle Crucis probably told the first Jack Tales in the area. They may have learned the tales from English or German ancestors or from other early settlers who had brought the stories from Europe.

McKeller "Kell" Harmon, late 1947 to early 1948

Cutliff's grandson Council Harmon (1807-1896), Sarah's grandfather, was born near the Watauga River. Council Harmon was a patriarch of Beech Mountain storytelling. As the father of 19 children and a stepchild by his second wife, Council delighted in sharing stories. (Some sources say he had 22 children.) He is described as funny and lively, a tall, slender man who spoke with a long drawl. (Harmon, Terry. *The Harmon Family, 1670 -1984: The Genealogy of Cutliff Harmon and His Descendants.* Boone, N.C.: Minor's Publishing Company, 1984.)

Orville has heard tales about Council Harmon. "He'd be coming down the road and meet someone. He'd sit down on a stump and start telling a story," Orville says.

"Council was run out of church for dancing. He promised the preacher he'd give up dancing, but he couldn't help himself. Every time he heard music, he started dancing."

Council Harmon and other mountain storytellers adapted European folktales to Appalachian settings. As in earlier tales, Appalachian Jack Tales often keep the king as a character, but he rocks on the porch of his mountain home. No throne for this king.

Council's son Kell Harmon (1863-1950) remained in the area and told stories to his children, including Sarah, mother of Orville. In turn, Orville listened and learned the stories Mama told. He shivered with her ghost tales, sharpened his cunning with her tales of clever Jack, and laughed with her riddles.

It's between Heaven and Earth, not on a tree.

Now I've told you, and you tell me. What is it?

(A knot on a tree)

A houseful, a yard full, but you can't catch a spoonful.

What is it?

(Smoke)

Sarah Hicks playfully challenged her children to listen carefully and to think. Orville remembers many of her lines.

"Mama'd say to us, 'If you can guess how many little pigs are in this sack, I'll give you both of them.' Or she'd say, 'Can you tell me what color old Joe's yellow turkey is?'

"Mama had a little rhyme for everything," Orville says. "We'd catch a ladybug and hold it on our hands, and she'd say, 'Ladybug, ladybug, fly away home....' About every time, the lady bug would fly off."

Mama's rhymes entertained her children and kept them with her as they worked.

I had a little dog and his name was Jack.
I tied his tail to the railroad track....

I had a little pony and his name was Jack,
I rode on his belly to save his back....

Before Orville was born, folktale collector Richard Chase had traveled through the Appalachian Mountains. Chase was searching for ballads and traditional songs, but on Beech Mountain, he also heard stories, including Jack Tales. He recorded the stories and ballads of several members of the Hicks and Harmon families. Gold Hicks was leery of Chase's proposal to record Mama's stories, but kinfolk persuaded Daddy to consent to the outsider's request.

Stories told by Orville's mother, her father, and other Beech Mountain relatives are printed in Chase's popular books, *Jack Tales* (1943) and *Grandfather Tales* (1948).

Orville, too, gathered Mama's stories and songs, her rhymes and riddles. He kept them in his memory.

Daddy: Gold Hicks

(1910-1994)

Daddy *was strict, but he lived it.*
—Orville

Orville's father, Gold Hicks, was a son of preacher Manuel Hicks and Martha Ellen Presnell Hicks, who was part Cherokee. Orville claims his paternal grandfather was "stricter than Daddy." Gold grew up with strict ways and kept them. He scorned books, forbade playing cards, and insisted that his daughters wear skirts that reached toward their ankles. Like his father, he became an unlicensed preacher. Gold Hicks preached at Bethany Baptist Church on Beech Mountain, and he preached at prayer meetings in homes nearby.

"Daddy didn't drive, never had a driver's license, never owned a car, and never needed to," Orville says.

For about two years, Gold and his brother-in-law, Adie Harmon, built roads with the Works Progress Administration, WPA, in Morganton. He earned $1.50 for a day's labor.

"Daddy'd get up real early in the morning and walk eight or ten miles to catch a ride to work. He'd stay in Morganton all week.

"We couldn't wait until Friday evening to meet Daddy because he always brought a poke of stick candy home with him for us to divide out. We would lick on the stick of candy some, then wrap it up and put it away for a while. We had to make it last us for the week."

After leaving the WPA job, Daddy worked at home, tending the family farm. He plowed and planted the garden, cut wood, and cared for the farm animals.

"A lot of people had by-words. Daddy's was 'buddy, buddy,'" Orville says.

"Buddy, buddy, let me tell you...," Gold Hicks would say, and people listened.

Despite his stern nature, Daddy had a gentle, caring side. When food was limited, he would see that his children had food first. Those days, he would head out for a day's work after eating only a piece of cornbread or a biscuit dipped in coffee.

Daddy didn't want visitors to leave his home hungry. He always made sure they ate before they left. "Sarah, open up another jar or two," he would say when company came.

"Daddy was always throwing a quilt on you while you were sleeping," Orville says. "You'd wake up and find out that he'd come in and put more cover on to keep you warm."

Orville remembers one cold night when temperatures dropped below ten degrees. He had a new puppy that he had put in the woodshed for the night. "About one o'clock in the morning, I heard Daddy slip out of the house and take a quilt to wrap up that little puppy. He couldn't stand the thought of that puppy out in the cold.

"Everyone thought the world of Daddy," Orville says. "Folks said if more people were like Gold Hicks, the world would be a better place.

"People say he ran the bootleggers out of that part of the mountains. He was tough—but he always had that little grin."

Neighbors called him "Honest Gold," and he passed that honesty to his children.

"Daddy got a new saw blade," Orville tells, "and somehow, Mary and Jerry and I broke it. Daddy found it and asked who broke it. Nobody said anything. Then he said, 'I wasn't going to whip who did it. I just wanted to give him a quarter.' We all said we'd done it, and nobody got a whipping."

The family of Manuel and Martha Ellen Presnell Hicks.
The young boy is Orville's daddy, Gold.

Daddy with granddaughter
JoAnn, Charlie's daughter

Bethany Baptist Church

Gold Hicks taught his sons the skills they needed to live in the mountains. One time, Orville and his brother Willis went squirrel hunting with their daddy. Not knowing a squirrel was overhead, Daddy stopped under the tree. Orville, with gun in hand, was ready for a squirrel just the same. Suddenly, the squirrel jumped down on Daddy's chest. Daddy was in quite a dither over the squirrel until the boys eventually wrangled the squirrel off him.

Orville's brother chided, "You're not afraid of that squirrel, are you?"

"No," his daddy replied, "but I thought Orville was going to shoot the squirrel with it still on me!"

Squirrels were common in the woods, but rocks were even more plentiful. Some of them were valuable.

"Daddy was always expecting to find a diamond somewhere," Orville says with a chuckle. "We'd see him coming across the hill of the evening, and we'd tell Mama, 'Daddy's coming. Better get supper ready.' Thirty minutes later we'd look back, and he'd hardly moved. He was looking at rocks.

"He'd say, 'We're rich, we're rich! I found a diamond! We don't have nothing to worry about now!' I bet he had a thousand diamonds when he died—every one of them quartz."

While Daddy collected his diamonds, Orville gathered stories of family life—jewels of a different sort.

Old Bethany Baptist Church

THE HOMEPLACE

If that house was still there today, it would be like a postcard.
It was so beautiful.
—Orville

From the 1930s to the 1950s, Orville's parents accumulated about 190 acres and a house between Beech Mountain and Valle Mountain. Orville's home sat in a hollow between hillsides. The peak of Rocky Face, with its stony outcropping, stood tall across the hollow from the house.

"It was a "big ol' two-story house," Orville says. It had two bedrooms downstairs, along with a kitchen and sitting room. The upstairs held storage space where Orville and the other children played when weather kept them inside.

Orville recalls the lullaby of night rain on the tin roof. "You'd hear that rain beating down. Next thing you'd know, you'd be asleep."

The house was not airtight, and sawdust insulation let the winter cold creep in. "After a big snow at night, we'd wake up and find an inch of snow on the bed."

To stay warm at night, Orville would snuggle under the feather tick. "The feather tick was like a big old quilt with feathers in it," says Orville. "Mama made it, or maybe her mama."

The house nestled against a slope. Rock posts supported a porch that wrapped around three sides and formed a sheltered hideout for children's play. The family gathered on the porch to snap beans or tie galax bunches, to talk, and to hear Mama's stories.

In a landscape of green hues, Rocky Face
rose above the home in the hollow.

The cellar held Mama's jars of vegetables and preserves. It also held durable produce from the garden: potatoes, onions, turnips and pumpkins. The house sat uphill to the right.

"We had poles over the porch that held up the roof. I'd hang on to those poles and swing from one to another all the way around the house," Orville says.

Daddy stacked hay in the fields near the house. The haystacks invited the children to climb. Orville and the other children had no shortage of places to play and to let their imaginations run free.

Everyone worked in the big garden, which produced food for the family and some extra to sell. Daddy plowed with Prince, the work horse. Orville and his brothers dug potatoes. Mama and the children picked beans.

"We had buildings for everything," Orville says. Daddy stored fertilizer and bean dust in the dust building. The dust protected the bean crop from the hungry and destructive bean-beetle larvae. The chicken house sheltered their chickens. Mama and Mary gathered fresh eggs there every evening.

When Daddy and the boys harvested corn at summer's end, they filled the corn crib with food for the livestock. A tool for shelling corn sat in the corner of the corn crib. "We used the corn sheller to knock the dried corn off the cob, and we'd feed the corn to the animals."

The smoke house attached to the corn crib. After hog-killing time in the fall, Daddy smoked the ham there and stored it for winter use.

Before cold weather came, Orville and his brothers helped stack firewood in the woodshed. The firewood warmed the house and fueled the kitchen stove, where Mama cooked potatoes and greens and baked cornbread and pumpkin pies. The family gathered around the big table in the kitchen to share the meals she prepared from homegrown food.

The cellar, built onto the side of the hill, stored produce from the garden. Daddy filled bins in the cellar with potatoes, pumpkins, onions, and apples. Mama canned food from the garden and then stacked her jars on shelves in the cellar. A room over the cellar also stored pumpkins.

The "'tater bin" was a little room built off the kitchen. Mama kept some potatoes, a jug of water, and a crock of pickled beans there. On cold days, she could go to the potato bin without walking out to the cellar to get food.

"We had a spring box instead of a spring house," Orville says. Spring water ran into the box and made a cool place to keep milk and butter. The spring uphill from the house supplied water for the family; they had no running water and no plumbing.

Mama's "bubby bush" grew by the spring. Girls sometimes wore the fragrant flowers on a string like a necklace. Sweet shrub and Carolina allspice are other names for the bush.

"That spring never did go dry, no matter how dry the weather was," Orville says. "We dipped spring water with a bucket and carried it to the house. We made sure we had two buckets at nighttime 'cause in the morning, Mama'd use one bucket for cooking and we'd have the other one to drink.

"We had a bubby bush beside the spring. You could rub it between your fingers and smell it." Orville rubs his fingers together and lifts them to his nose. He smiles as he recalls the delicious strawberry-like scent of the deep red flower.

Home was a haven of love and a place of beauty. Mama planted flowers in the yard—both wild and cultivated flowers. She had a snowball bush and red and yellow roses. Apple trees bloomed in pale pink-white and filled the spring air with fragrance. Currant bushes and grape vines grew in the yard, and blueberry and huckleberry bushes on the hill bore fruit. Mama and the children filled pails with summer berries the family would eat all year.

Huckleberries grew on the hill and bore tiny fruit.

A branch ran beside the house and across the road to make a little waterfall. "A branch is smaller than a creek," says Orville. "We'd play in the branch, and sometimes we found an arrowhead in it. I guess it washed down the mountain. We'd find some in the field there too.

"We had a path that went right past the corn building and the chicken building and on to the outhouse," Orville says. "Beside the path was the prettiest maple tree I've seen in my life. I remember the leaves in the fall of the year. We'd pile them up and hide in them. It was a beautiful big old maple tree. Gosh, it was that big around." Orville stretches his arms in a wide circle. His blue eyes twinkle.

"Could have been a little touch of heaven around that maple tree."

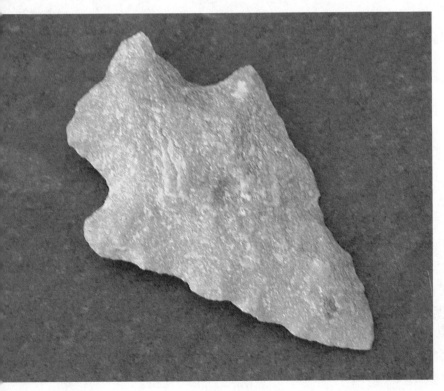

Orville found arrowheads like this one found by his cousin Leonard Harmon at nearby Cove Creek. The arrowheads hint of stories from earlier mountain life.

Although electricity had been lighting other homes on the mountain since 1947, Daddy didn't consent to getting electricity until 1964. Orville was thirteen years old. When the first light bill came, Orville says Daddy probably didn't sleep that night for worrying.

"I don't know how we're going to pay that light bill," Daddy said. "Looks like we'll have to have the lights took out."

"We're going to have to pull a lot of herbs to pay that three-dollar light bill," Orville's brother said.

Orville, Mary, and Jerry headed to the hills, where they gathered herbs to help Daddy pay the bill.

When a lightbulb broke, Orville says his daddy wouldn't turn on the lights. "He thought he might get electrocuted. It took three days to get a light man to look at it."

After connecting to electricity, the Hicks family got a refrigerator. Except for lights, which Daddy turned off about an hour after dark, the refrigerator was the only concession to electrical use. Mama still cooked on her wood stove.

Orville's home provides the setting for many of his stories. "When I was growing up, we used to sell pumpkins out at the barn," he says as he begins his tale of the mule eggs.

Jerry, Orville, and Mary pose during an outing to Cherokee.

LIFE ON THE MOUNTAIN

I was brought up hard, but I loved every minute of it. Mama and Daddy was the best parents. There was a lot of love in our family.
—Hattie Hicks Presnell, sister of Orville

Orville's family seldom ventured far beyond their home in the mountain hollow. "We didn't need to," says Orville. "We had what we needed. We'd grow our own food. We hunted and picked berries."

Sometimes they went down to Valle Crucis to the Mast Store or to the bean market in West Jefferson. Beech Mountain was full of kinfolk, and Orville's family walked to visit them. They walked to church and to each other's houses for prayer meetings, often on Friday or Saturday nights.

"I remember going to a lot of prayer meetings at Uncle Monroe's house," Orville says. Monroe Harmon was Mama's brother.

"If we got a mile from the house, we thought we'd gone somewhere." Boone was only about fifteen miles away, but to Orville, Boone may as well have been New York.

Just once, Orville's family ventured to Cherokee, North Carolina. The trip was a treat from Orville's sister Hattie and her husband, Bennie Presnell.

"We camped by the road," Orville says. "Mama, Hattie, and Mary slept in the car. Me and Bennie and Daddy and Jerry built a campfire and camped on the ground beside the car."

Links to the world beyond the mountains were few. The family had a battery-powered radio, but they had no television. Daddy limited what Orville and the family could listen to on the radio. "We didn't hear about war or about drugs," Orville says.

While Gold and Sarah Hicks welcomed visitors to their home, the shy but curious children kept their distance. "We young'uns would hide behind the couch and peep out. Daddy'd say, 'Come out here,' and we'd say, 'No,' and hide back down."

Mornings began long before sunlight filtered into the hollow. "Daddy usually got up and had the fire built around five o'clock. The rest of us got up about five-thirty or six. He'd have the fire built and the kitchen warm by the time we got up."

Mama and Daddy both worked in the big garden, as did the children. Everyone got up early. Daddy would say just once, "Hit the field," and his children knew he meant business. No one said, "No, I'm not going."

Despite the mountain terrain, the Hicks family harvested ample food supplies from their garden. "I expect we'd eat twenty-five to thirty bushels of potatoes in a year," Orville says. "Mama'd put up fifteen hundred to two thousand cans of food." When the family needed food, they went to the cellar, not to the store.

During the summer, Mama and the children picked wild strawberries, blueberries, and elderberries. They also picked huckleberries from a big patch on the hilltop.

Orville remembers trying to fill his pail with huckleberries. "They were so little, it'd take a long time to get much. Of course, I ate my share of them."

Fall was a busy time at the mountain farm—harvesting produce from the garden, smoking hog meat, and selling the ham downhill in Valle Crucis.

"I always liked the fall of the year," Orville says. "We'd dig 'taters. I liked to see how many we'd get from a row.

"Sometimes in the fall of the year we'd go up on top of Beech Mountain and gather hazelnuts. We'd pile in the back of Hassell's truck—me and Mary and Jerry and Hassell's boys, Ronnie and Sylvester and Monty. We'd fill big old sacks with hazelnuts. Sometimes we stayed overnight and camped outside the truck."

Later, Orville and his family would sit by the fire and crack hazelnuts. Mama baked the nuts in cookies.

Some days after Orville had dug potatoes or picked beans, he would hunt in the evening. The woods were generous in providing for the Hicks family's needs, and the Hickses knew well how to glean what the mountains offered.

Orville's sister Hattie
and her husband, Bennie Presnell

With forty to fifty chickens around the farm, little chicks were always skittering about. Orville calls the chicks "diddles." "When we young'uns got close to the diddles, the hens would peck us, and we'd call for Mama."

"We had a good milk cow," says Orville. Milking was usually his chore. "I'd bring the milk up to Mama, and she'd strain it through a white rag into a gallon jar. Then, she'd carry the milk to the spring box." Cool water from the mountain spring chilled the milk and kept it fresh.

Mama used cream that separated from the milk to make butter. "We had a wood churn, and we all liked to churn butter. We took turns—me and Mary and Jerry. Sometimes Mama shook the cream in a jug until it turned to butter, and she'd tell us a tale while she did it."

Along with cows and chickens, the family raised two hogs each year. Fall was hog-killing time. "The little young'uns would play with the hog bladder—like in *Little House in the Big Woods*—not even knowing what it was at the time."

Orville's strict father had not let many books in the house, except the Bible and schoolbooks. Orville had brought Laura Ingalls Wilder's books home from school to read.

Later, Orville and his daddy took "hog ham" to the Mast Store in Valle Crucis. Sometimes a brother went along too. They carried the ham as they walked the five miles down to the store. Orville was always glad to reach "the half-way log," where Daddy let them stop to rest. At the store, they traded ham for flour, sugar, and winter shoes.

"The walk back was about straight up. Daddy'd say, 'Make it to the half-way log and you can rest again.'"

In March of 1960, a blizzard blanketed the mountains in snow. Repeated storms over several weeks piled snow deeply and drifted to depths of eighteen feet. "We dug a tunnel to the spring box and one to the cellar so we could get food from it."

A helicopter dropped a sack of food that sank into the snow. Orville's family dug the food out with a shovel. The sack included not only staple food but also candy bars. To the Hicks children, this was a rare treat. Outsiders thought the mountain folk were hungry since they couldn't get out to a store; however, the snow posed fewer challenges for the hardy mountain family than it did for many other people. Mama had canned enough vegetables from the garden to last through winter. Just the same, the family appreciated the food, and the children were thrilled to get the candy bars.

One cold, snowy evening, Orville's family had some unexpected visitors. Orville was about six or seven years old.

"I hear something outside," Mama said. "Something's come up on the porch."

"There's nothing out there," Daddy answered, "but if there is, we'll find it in the morning."

"In the morning," Orville says, "we found about a hundred of our neighbor's sheep—all huddled on the porch to get out of the wind and snow. It took Mama days to get the porch cleaned off."

Candy dropped from the sky and a porch filled with refugee sheep—such memories surely linger with a mountain boy.

Ray Hicks and his children Ted and Cathy plowed the rocky slopes with a horse (1964), as did Orville's family.

Gilbert and Frank Carswell of Burke County plowed with a mule. Orville recalls his family's temperamental mule and their corn crib, much like the building pictured.

IN THE FIELD

Okay, young'uns, get to bed early
so you can get up early to hit the field.
—Daddy

The Hicks family's garden lay on a slope and, like much mountain land, was scattered with rocks. Through the years, Daddy moved rocks. Using the sled behind the horse or mule, he carried stones away from the garden and piled them nearby.

As Daddy and the boys worked in the field, Mama brought them milk and cornbread to eat. "That way we could work all day and wouldn't have to go back to the house to eat," Orville says.

"We had two horses at one time, but later, when there weren't so many of us at home, we just had one. Prince was a big friendly horse. You could walk under him or get on his back. He wouldn't hurt nothing. When we worked in that lower field, we'd ride him down to the creek to let him drink water, and we'd ride him back to the field.

"The horse pulled a disc through the field to break up the dirt, and we'd pull a harrow through to make it smooth and take the lumps out. The harrow had teeth on it. We used a horse to pull the mowing scythe too. Daddy used to mow his hay with it. Then we had a hay rake."

Prince pulled the heavy wooden sled in the garden when the family gathered crops. The horse served as tractor and truck. "The young'uns drove him up the field to gather a load of potatoes," Orville says. Riding on the sled behind the horse was a treat for Orville and the other children.

Years later, Daddy had a mule that pulled the plow and the sled. Orville's recollections of the mule are tainted by a frightening encounter when he was about ten years old. After working in the field one day, Orville bent over the corn box as he shelled some corn to feed the mule. The ungrateful mule reached over and bit Orville on the back of the neck.

"I ran to the chicken house," Orville said, "but the mule followed me and cornered me there. That old mule showed his teeth just like he was laughing at me."

Orville is sure the mule knew he had the upper hand over a boy. Daddy came to Orville's rescue.

When a wild animal later attacked the mule and killed it, Orville felt no sadness. "But Daddy nearly cried," says Orville. "He'd paid three hundred dollars for that mule."

The garden mostly provided food for the family, but they planted enough beans to sell. "We never grew tobacco. Daddy thought tobacco was sinful," Orville says.

Through the year, the Hicks family bought necessary items on credit at Mast Store. When the bean crop came in, they paid their debt. The Hickses grew "shelly beans" as their main cash crop. "Shelly beans are long and striped real pretty with red," Orville explains.

Orville's brother Hassell had a truck. He drove Daddy, Orville, and Jerry the forty miles to West Jefferson, where they would sell their beans at the bean market.

"That was a big treat, going to West Jefferson. We'd ride in the back of the truck."

Once when they were preparing to go to the market, Orville's brother picked out the best beans, put them in a "sample sack," and tied a red ribbon around it. When they got to the bean market, the proprietor asked to see a sample.

Young Orville piped up. "Do you want to see the one my brother tied with the red ribbon?"

"No. Give me another one," the man said.

"He bought them anyway," Orville recalls. "They were pretty beans. They brought pretty good, if I remember."

Once on a return drive from West Jefferson, the headlights on the truck went out. Hassell stopped and bought two flashlights. Orville and his nephew Ronnie lay on the fender of the truck and held the flashlights, lighting the narrow, winding road to home.

"We went real slow," says Orville. "That was a long ride!"

"One time we raised popcorn," Orville says. "We was plowing the field, and it got so hot the corn started popping."

Sometimes a glimmer in Orville's blue eyes reveals where fact ends and fiction begins.

"The old mule thought it was snow, and he just lay down and froze to death."

Several apple trees grew around the Hickses' home. Among the trees were a Virginia Beauty tree that Daddy had grafted and also a Wolf River tree, an old apple variety. Orville's family had a pound apple tree too, which produced large, tough-skinned apples. "They're good winter apples," says Orville.

Early in Orville's school years, he told his teacher that he had a pineapple growing at his house.

"I'd like to see that pineapple," the teacher said with disbelief.

The next day, Orville took his prize apple to school.

"Oh, that's a pound apple," the teacher explained.

Orville had misunderstood the name.

As Orville grew up on the farm in the hollow, he learned his lessons about pound apples, potatoes, and ornery mules, and he also gathered farming lore, stories that were earthy and fertile.

Orville looks at a hand plow that his cousin Ray Hicks used. Orville's family used a hand plow like this to cut a furrow.

Orville's mother used an older cast iron wood stove similar to Rosa Hicks's enameled one. A wood-fed fire beneath the burners makes heat for cooking. Smoke rises through a pipe at the top of the stove and escapes through a vent to the outside.

CANNING AND PREPARING FOR WINTER

We'd better get enough wood in to keep that stove a-burning
so we can do the canning on it.
—Mama

Every summer, Mama washed her collection of jars in a big tin wash tub. "She'd bought it new just for canning. She canned beans, pumpkin, corn, sweet peas, and mustard greens. Not everybody canned roastin' ears, but Mama did." Orville relished the savory taste. He remembers sneaking into the cellar and eating corn that Mama had canned.

Mama canned the ripe berries the family picked. She made huckleberry preserves, strawberry jam, and wild currant jelly. Once a year Mama bought peaches from a man who traveled through the mountains. She gave each of her children one fresh peach to eat. The rest she canned for winter.

"Mama had a big Home Comfort stove," Orville says. "The whole stove was cast iron and black. It didn't have that white enamel around it."

Mama also dried apple slices and bean pods for winter use. She threaded them on a string and hung them in the attic or behind the stove to dry. Later she cooked the dried apples and beans with water for winter meals.

Orville's family kept three or four beehives. The children liked to watch as Daddy collected honey from the hives. "We'd always come back with a few bee stings, and we'd run to Mama. 'Mama, Mama, I got bee stung.' She'd say, 'I told you young'uns not to go down there.'"

When Daddy "robbed the hive," he wore a jacket made from an old quilt. A wire frame supported the covering for his head. Daddy filled the hive with smoke from burning rags. The smoke ran the bees out so he could reach the honey safely.

Some years he got sourwood honey, some years locust honey—"whatever the bees gathered that year," says Orville. Sourwood trees grew abundantly in the mountains around Orville's home. Honey made from sourwood nectar is prized for its flavor.

Fingerlike clusters of white flowers draw honeybees to sourwood trees.

"Each beehive held four or five sashes," Orville says. "A sash is a wooden frame. It notches in there and the bees build their honeycomb around that. Daddy'd leave a sash in each bee gum so the bees could get by through the winter.

"Sometimes bees would leave the hive and swarm," says Orville. "Daddy'd beat on a wash pan. For a long time I didn't know why he did that, but the bees would hear a racket and they'd land. One time they landed on a limb. It looked like a washtub full of bees. Daddy cut the limb and carried it back to the hive.

"Sometimes we found a bee tree out in the woods. One time I was walking and found a big one, and we got about three washtubs of honey out of it. That was a lot of honey."

When Daddy traded hog ham at Mast Store, he would get a twenty-five-pound sack of sugar. "That'll have to last us all winter," he'd say. Sugar was limited, but honey came freely. Mama made jellies with honey, and Orville drizzled it over oatmeal and biscuits.

Whenever Daddy was out, he would pick up fallen branches or trunks of small trees that had fallen. "Sometimes Mama'd hitch the sled to Prince and go all over the mountain," Orville says. "She'd pick up pine stumps, dead wood, and branches about the size of your arm. We'd use that for kindling. She'd pick up a little here, then go a little farther, and pretty soon the sled was full."

By the time he was seven, Orville helped his father and brothers gather wood. Before winter set in, they took the horse or mule and sled on top of the mountain. They picked up dead wood for kindling, but for winter heat they cut harder wood: oak, cherry, locust, maple, and hickory.

"We used a cross-cut saw," says Orville. "Daddy'd get on one end, and Jerry and I'd take turns on the other end."

Prince and the sled did the work of a truck. The strong horse pulled sled loads of wood downhill to the woodshed. "When we had long poles, Daddy'd hook a chain around them, and Prince would pull it on down the mountain. Sometimes when we'd pull a log off the hill, Daddy'd put us up on top of the horse, and we'd ride on down the hill."

With the harvest in and the cellar full, the family gathered around a warm fire, where Mama spun tales for cold evenings.

The Christmas of "the nickel cap buster." Daddy made the sloped bench to seat children of various sizes at the kitchen table.

Back row: Ronnie, Mary, Sylvester, Orville, Jerry.

Front row: Monty, Billy Presnell, Brenda, Bobby, Richard.

CHRISTMAS

Here it is nearly Christmas and we haven't got nothing.
What're we going to do?
—Mama

Christmas was lean for the Hicks family. Candy bars and sodas were rare treats, but the children got them at Christmas. "That's about all we got," Orville says. "Sometimes we got a piece of stick candy or an orange."

Orville remembers one Christmas when he was very young. The family had little money to spend, but Mama used her ingenuity. She wrapped a spoonful of sugar in a white rag and dipped the rag in milk as a treat for each child to suck on. Orville's memory of his mother is sweet, just like the treats she created.

"Sometimes Mama made gingerbread cookies," Orville says. "I made them too. I'd take a lump of dough and press it with a spoon to shape the head and arms and legs."

For a while, Orville's brother Charlie lived in Siler City. No one expected Charlie to drive the long road home one Christmas, but he made his way to Beech Mountain in the snow—and then got stuck just below the cellar as he tried to climb the hill with his car.

"We were so tickled to see someone coming," Orville says. "He brought me a little red wagon. The next day, Daddy took Prince, his big old horse, and pulled Charlie's car out of the snow."

In 1957, Daddy had saved enough money to buy toys for the children. He bought a battery powered tractor for Jerry and a bulldozer for Orville. "It had a little light on top. We thought we was rich."

Gold Hicks allowed his family to have their first Christmas tree in 1961. They cut a white pine from the hillside above the house.

"Nancy and Gary brought candy canes to put on it. I couldn't wait to take the tree down so we could eat the candy canes." The memory brings out Orville's easy laughter.

Daddy got a "nickel cap buster" and a roll of caps for the boys that year.

"That was the only time we had caps," Orville says. Afterward, the boys made their own sound effects for the toy guns.

Those were the abundant years.

As in earlier years, kinfolk gathered with buckets, dishpans, and shovels to clear the three miles of road from Rominger to Matney after the blizzard of 1993. Third from the left is Orville's brother Charlie.

CARING WAYS

We helped each other out. When I worked in the Banner Elk Hospital before I was married, I bought enough milk for the twins to last a month. Mama nursed them, but she didn't have enough milk for both of them.
—Hattie Hicks Presnell

As Orville grew, he saw models of gentleness in his stern but caring father and in his nurturing mother. Orville learned their gentle ways.

When Orville was about ten years old, the milk cow got away. The brothers went looking for her. They found her on top of the mountain, where she'd given birth to twin calves; but the cow abandoned one.

"We took turns carrying the calves down the mountain," Orville says. "They looked so much alike, I couldn't tell them apart."

But the mother cow could. Daddy had to hold her to keep her from attacking the unclaimed calf while it nursed. Even though the mother never accepted the second calf, it thrived with the extra care the Hickses gave it.

Orville's family had a collie they called Old Shep. Once when Daddy was mowing, he disturbed a rabbits' nest. The mowing scythe accidentally struck the mother rabbit, leaving a nest of orphaned bunnies.

"Old Shep would get one rabbit in his mouth and carry it a ways till that little rabbit made a racket. He set it down. Then he picked it up again and took it to the house." Old Shep carried the bunnies, one by one, until he had brought all four to safety.

In turn, Mama took care of the little rabbits. She fed them with an eyedropper. Later, Old Shep and the bunnies drank milk together from the dish Mama set on the porch. When the bunnies grew enough to take care of themselves, Mama set them free in the yard.

Families on the mountain looked out for each other too.

"We kept a milk cow," Orville says, "and we'd give Hassell three or four gallons of milk every week. Then Hassell'd help us pick up potatoes when we dug them. Their young'uns would come too. We'd like that 'cause we'd get to see them.

"When it snowed, Daddy wanted us to shovel out the road just in case anyone had to get out. With all of us, it didn't take very long.

"There was so many of us. About the only time we really needed help was at hog killing time."

"I guess Mama and Daddy just had a love for other people.
If Daddy knew somebody was sick, or Mama, they'd walk ten miles to help them—if it was a stranger or a friend," Orville says.

One time Mama was getting ready to take medicine to an uncle in the next hollow. Orville was young but wanted to go. "I'll walk," he promised, so Mama consented.

Daddy warned, "Now, you be sure to get back before dark."

On the way home, snow started to fall. At the creek, they heard a panther scream.

"It scared me and Mama to death," Orville says. "Mama picked me up and ran toward the house, but the panther jumped on the fence right in front of us. The panther screamed. Mama was so scared that she dropped me. She screamed too. That must have scared the panther 'cause it ran off. Then Mama picked me up and took off to the house."

Orville has remembered the often-told story of how his frightened mama scared away the panther, and he has remembered the sound of a panther's scream. But what's more, he remembers the gentle and generous ways of his parents, who showed him how to live.

A Silver-spotted Skipper. "The yard is full of Oh Susiannahs. You'd better go out there and see if you can catch some."

A Time for Play

Red Rover, Red Rover, send Mary right over.
—From the children's game Red Rover

When Orville was little, one of the children caught a mouse. "We made a pet out of it and kept it in a cage," Orville says. "Daddy made a little harness out of leather and put a little sled on it. We watched the mouse pull it across the floor. But then Mama's cat got the mouse, sled and all, and ran off with it."

The hollow around Orville's home was a natural arena for childhood play. Flowers in the yard attracted butterflies. "Mama'd come in and say, 'The yard is full of Oh Susiannahs. You'd better go out there and see if you can catch some.'"

Imagination thrived as the children created trucks and tractors from whatever was at hand. "Sometimes we'd get a big old stick of wood and put wheels on it. If we didn't have anything else to use, we'd use a rock and push it around." The addition of motor sounds was all that was needed.

The big porch at Orville's home was a favorite place for children's play. Orville enjoyed driving his toy bulldozer in the dirt under the porch. Jerry joined him with his toy tractor. When Daddy had bought the toys as Christmas gifts, they had batteries; but the batteries soon wore out. Then Orville and Jerry just pushed their toys. Even on rainy days, Orville and the other children played on the big porch or in the dirt beneath it.

"We'd get dirty playing under the porch, and Mama'd say, 'I know where them young'uns have been—under the porch.'"

The big room upstairs offered another play place, especially on rainy days. "We couldn't hardly hear ourselves talk for the rain beating on the tin roof," Orville recalls.

Mama had old clothes stored upstairs, and Orville and the other children pulled them out to play with.

"Sometimes playing in the attic was a little scary," he says, "because we'd think we heard a ghost." Not wanting ghostly playmates, the children would run downstairs.

In the evening as the children played in a patch of woods by the yard, Mama would call them in. They may have been reluctant to end their play, but when Mama called out, "Hocus Pocus is down there in the woods," the children scampered back to the house, lickety-split.

The children made a playground of the field and the haystacks. One of the children would climb to the top of a haystack and grab the pole that extended above the top of the hay. The others tried to pull that child off the hay. "Whoever could stay on would be king or queen of the haystack," Orville says, "but when some of the sisters got you by the hair, you'd come down from there!"

The children played other games too, including Red Rover, London Bridge, and Bum, Bum, Bum. Sometimes they made up their own games, using what was at hand. They rolled car tires, and they slid down the snowy mountain on an old car hood.

The boys used inner tubes from car tires to make slingshots. "I'd tie a strip of rubber to a fork cut out of a laurel bush," says Orville. "Now that red rubber'd shoot a rock like a bullet. Black rubber wouldn't shoot half as hard."

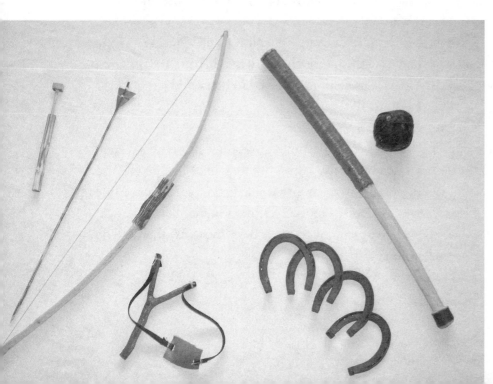

The children in Orville's family made playthings from what was at hand. They played with horseshoes right off the horse and toys like these handcrafted by Orville: popgun, bow and arrow, slingshot, and ball and bat.

49

Orville and his brothers played softball too. He used a bat carved from the trunk of a straight tree. "Oak and ash make good bats," says Orville.

Though he had no ball, that didn't stop Orville from playing. He just made a ball by wrapping a tin can with strips of inner-tube rubber. "Sometimes the metal cut through the rubber and cut our hands, but we just kept on playing," Orville says. "We'd be out the next day playing again."

For Gold Hicks, playing checkers might as well have been gambling. Once a teacher gave the Hicks children a checkers game.

"When Daddy saw us playing with it, he throwed it in the fire. The next day, he walked all the way to the school and told the teacher not to give us anything like that again."

Orville and his brothers used to poke a stick through an apple and sling the stick so the apple would fly off the end. They wanted to see how far the apple would go. Once Orville stuck a potato on a stick and swung. The potato flew through the air—but not in the direction he intended. Instead, the potato hit his father.

"Daddy caught me after I tore down about an acre of corn," Orville says with a laugh. "He told me, 'I'm not going to whip you for hitting me in the head, but I am going to whip you for wasting food.'"

For a long time, Orville and the other children didn't have a bicycle. Finally, when Orville's cousins offered to sell them a bicycle, Daddy agreed to let his boys trade a BB gun for the bike. "But if one of you gets hurt on it, that bicycle's going to go," Daddy warned.

The bike had a broken handlebar. Sure enough, Orville wrecked on the bike and punctured his abdomen with the rough, rusty handlebar. "I was scared Daddy was going to take the bicycle away from us. I said to Mary and Jerry, 'Don't tell. Don't tell.' It's a wonder I didn't die."

Horseshoe pitching was a favorite pastime on Sunday afternoons. "Back then we had little horseshoes—right off the horse—not big ones like people use now," Orville explains. Groups of fifteen to twenty would gather at the horseshoe pits by Old Tough Road, close to Daddy's brother Luther's home. When he was young, Orville watched the older boys and men pitch horseshoes. By the time he was ten or eleven, he pitched too.

Orville takes a swing with a homemade bat and ball like ones he played with as a boy.

"I've seen them get down with a straw to measure. I mean it was serious!"

He also pitched at Ray's house with Ray and his sons, Ted and Leonard. "Ray called a wringer a 'nickel.' He'd raise his long arms and yell, 'Hey, I got a nickel.' Sometimes a horseshoe would go rolling off and someone would say, 'That one still had the horse on it.'"

For Orville, homespun fun brought as much delight as any store-bought entertainment could. "We never lacked for things to play with," he says as he slips a loop of string in and out of his fingers to make a crow's foot. "We had a lot of things to loll away the hours."

RAY HICKS

Gawd!
—Ray Hicks

Orville shared Hicks ancestry with his older cousin Ray and Harmon ancestry with Ray's wife, Rosa. Rosa's father and Orville's mother were brother and sister. Orville's reflections on boyhood and Ray turn to stories, weekend haircuts, and digging potatoes.

"Ray's home was three miles away if you followed the road," Orville says, "more like a mile if you walked up and across the mountain."

Ray and Rosa had five children. Orville, Jerry, and Willis looked forward to Ray's coming, knowing that Ray and his sons often brought a "funny book."

Big Ray and Rosa; Ray's home on Beech Mountain

Orville and his brothers knew their daddy wouldn't allow comic books in the house, so they hid the books. When the cousins returned, the boys swapped books.

Later, Orville hunted with Ray's son Ted. The two boys loved the woods, where they observed wildlife, herbs, and trees. They also cut wood together, pitched horseshoes, and played card games, including Setback. The boys were like brothers.

"I thought the world of Ray," Orville says. "He was like a second dad."

Ray told tales and shared his front porch philosophy and mountain wisdom with all who listened. Even as a child, Orville noticed something special about the way Ray spoke.

"When Ray told a story, he'd look right straight at me, no matter how many other people were there—like he was telling the tale just to me."

Even then, Ray hoped young Orville would be a keeper of stories.

GHOSTS AND NIGHT BEASTS ON THE MOUNTAIN

*Mama'd tell stories about Old Tough Road.
I'd be scared to death sometimes when I'd be out there hunting.*
—Orville

As Orville gathered his stories, he collected a few shivers.

Orville was six years old when Daddy brought a puppy home in his pocket. The little feist, Brownie, would be Orville's companion for fifteen years. "He went everywhere with me," Orville says.

When Orville was a young teen, he was walking with Brownie near the gristmill below his house. "Brownie started growling and hid under my legs like he was scared to death," says Orville. That's when Orville saw an old man walking with a cane.

"He went into the bushes, but the bushes didn't move. I think I beat the dog home after that," Orville says with a laugh. When he got home, he was afraid to say anything about the odd experience. Finally, he spoke.

"Well, I saw that too," Daddy said.

Orville tells of when Mama heard a ghost: "She was gathering herbs on Old Tough Road, and she heard a team of horses and a wagon coming down through there. She told the young'uns to get out of the way, and she got them up on the bank. She heard a lot of racket and the bushes was moving, but she never did see anything."

Such stories of Old Tough Road were plentiful. "Folks say the road was haunted because it was built on Sunday. 'Mama, Mama,' we'd say, 'tell us about Old Tough Road and the ghosts on it.'"

Ghost stories abounded in the hills and hollows around Beech Mountain. Many tales evolved from unexplained happenings, but others were traditional tales. Ghost tales not only entertained but also served as words of caution for children.

The darkness of the unlit mountain nights posed its own threats. "Walking in the dark was scary," Orville says. When he walked the half mile uphill to his brother Hassell's house, Mama would tell him to come back home before dark.

One summer night, he was returning from his sister Hattie's home. "I heard something beside me in the woods," Orville says. "I ran; it'd run. I stopped; it'd stop. When I got to the bridge, it stopped. Folks say a ghost won't cross water."

Another night, Orville was walking back home from his Uncle Adie Harmon's house. "I got to thinking about Russell Farthing's bull and started to run. Next thing I knew, I was seeing stars. I'd run smack-dab into that bull. The bull went one way up the creek, and I went the other way up the road about ninety miles an hour. I don't remember opening the gate. I must have gone over the top of it."

Night sounds on the mountain could be frightening too. "From the porch you could hear a panther scream up on Beech Mountain." Bobcats sometimes wailed all night long.

When Orville was young, his family had an eerie late-night visitor. "We'd gone to bed and had the lamps blowed out," says Orville. A strange sound awakened the family. He followed his father into the kitchen. Something big and dark jumped through the window and landed on the table, then jumped back out—a panther, they assumed.

Nowadays, eerie beasts and ghostly happenings leap and creep through Orville's stories—reflections of a mountain childhood filled with mystery.

Orville's family gathered shiny galax
leaves to sell to floral markets.

GATHERING HERBS

Herbs kept us going.
—Orville

While the farm provided for the Hickses' basic needs, native plants offered a valuable source of income for Orville's family.

Orville's first recollection of herb-gathering is of watching his mother leave with her burlap sacks. "I nearly cried, watching Mama go. I didn't want her to go off. I'd sit on the porch and watch for Mama to come back. She'd come home late in the afternoon with a big sack of galax on her back, about gived out.

"Sometimes Mama would bring us young'uns something from the mountain—a turtle or a little rabbit. Sometimes she brought us mountain tea [teaberry or wintergreen] to chew on."

Mama would come home after gathering herbs and say, "Bet I can make you young'uns say, 'Who.'"

"No, you can't either, Mama," the children would say.

"Well, I don't guess I can, but I know someone down the road who can," she'd say.

"Who, Mama? Who?" And she caught the children in her playful trap every time.

When Mama went herb-gathering, or wildcrafting as she would say, she always told the family where she was going. The hills and hollows all had names—Bear Wallow, Tom Thumb's Hollow, Rocky Face, Long Mountain, Dead-a-lock, Hickory Patch, and Old Tough Road.

When Orville was five, before he was old enough to gather herbs himself, he went along as Mama gathered. He would carry a burlap sack and follow her through the mountain hollows. As she worked, he played beside her. Sometimes he climbed trees or swung on vines.

Mama watched her little ones as she gathered. "Now don't you get out of my sight," she warned. In the afternoon when Mama had filled her sacks with herbs, Orville helped drag the sacks home.

By age seven or eight, Orville was gathering herbs alongside Mama. Mary, Jerry, Nancy, and Willis often went too. Before they hiked into the hollows, Mama packed cornbread and raw onion heads for their lunches. Sometimes Orville gathered herbs with Nancy and Willis instead of with Mama.

One day as Orville and Mama picked galax, they came upon a group of men and a moonshine still. The men had painted their faces black so they wouldn't be recognized. Orville and Mama crouched just out of sight and then quietly crept away. From then on, they would stay away from that part of the woods.

Orville's mother, along with others in the family, gathered galax and log moss to sell to Sluder Floral Company in Newland. Their galax would go to florists to make funeral wreaths. Mama and the children also gathered life plant, mayapple, and pink and yellow lady slippers. They dug roots of ginseng, bloodroot, and angelica, and they gathered leaves and bark from beadwood (witch hazel) and sassafras trees. They sold these roots, herbs, and barks to Mr. Wilcox at Wilcox Drug Company in Boone. In turn, he would resell the plant materials to companies that made medicines.

CASH PRICE LIST FOR ROOTS, HERBS, LEAVES, BARKS, ETC. DELIVERED

Angelica Root.....................40
Balmoney Leaves only,well dry....30
Balm of Gilead Buds, dry.........25
Bayberry Bark of Root............10
Beeswax, Yellow..................25
Beth Root........................15
Blackberry Bark of Root..........15
Black Cohost Root, bone dry......05
Black Haw Tree Bark, rossed......18
Black Haw Tree Bark, unrossed....13
Black Haw Bark of Root...........20
Blood Root, fibers on, dry.......25
Blue Cohosh Root, clean, dry.....05
Boneset Herb, cut up.............02
Burdock Root, clean..............15
Butterfly (True Pleurisy) Root..15
Catnip Herb, leafy, not cut up...
Catnip Leaves and short tops not
        over 4" long.............
Catnip Herb Green Stage..........03
Cotton Root Bark.................08
Deer Tongue Leaves...........20
Elder Flowers....................15
Gelsemium Root (Yellow Jasmine).08
Ginseng Root, wild..........Market
Golden Seal Root............Market
Horsenettle Root (Bullnettle)...08
Lady Slipper Root................85
Life Root Plant, bone dry.......03
Lobelia Herb, no roots, dry.....12
Log Moss.........................06
        (We will not buy this moss
        unless it is clean, dry,
        green color, in pieces not
        smaller than 1 foot square,
        larger pieces are better
        quality.)
Mayapple Root, clean.............25
Mullein Leaves, bright, dry.....02
Maypop Herb (Passion Flower)....08
Peppermint Leaves, whole, hand-
  picked,not broken up,nostems..20

Pleurisy Root....................15
Poke Root, bone dry..............03
Sarsaperilla Root, white, dry....10

SASSAFRAS BARK
Bark of Root, Natural............14
Bark of Root, Well rossed........35
Bark of Tree, Natural............02

Shonny Haw Root Bark, No Tree,...20
Shonny Haw Bush Bark, Natural....16
Slippery Elm Brk.Rossed White....10
Spearmint Leaves, Whole hand-
  picked no stems, not broken up
  no tops.......................20
Squaw Vine, bright...............11
Spikenard Root...................20
Star Grass Root, not tops........60
Star Root, dry...................60
Stone Root, cut up, must be dry
        or will not be accepted..05
Tansey Leaves, Bright............10
Wahoo Bark of Root...............50
Wahoo Bark of Tree...............15

WILD CHERRY BARK
Thin,Natural, no rough bark no
        wood, smooth.............05
Thin, Rossed.....................07
Thick, Natural...................02
Thick, Rossed....................04
Wild Cherries, dry, meaty........15

Witch Hazel Leaves,bright,dry,
        free of stems and balls..09
Witch Hazel Bark.................05
Wild Ginger Root, with fibers....20
Wild Indigo Root.................10
Wild Lettuce Leaves, dry, green..10
Wild Yam Root, with fibers, dry..03
Wintergreen Leaves, dry..........15
Wintergreen Herb.................05
Yellow Dock Root, no black tops,,05

We buy copper, brass, lead, zinc,
used car batteries, beef hides, tal-
low, fur, etc.,at highest market
price.

WILCOX DRUG COMPANY
BOONE, NORTH CAROLINA

ALL ABOVE PRICES ARE SUBJECT TO CHANGE WITHOUT NOTICE, ALL GOODS MUST
BE CLEAN AND DRY, UNLESS OTHERWISE STATED.

We are in the market for the following in October, November, and Dec-
ember. See us for contracts by late summer.

LAUREL (IVY) TIPS, WHITE PINE TIPS, HEMLOCK TIPS, BOXWOOD TIPS, BALSAM
SPRAYES & TIPS, PRINCESS PINE OR GROUND PINE.

North Carolina mountains have been a major source of ginseng for China, where ridgy ginseng roots are valued as a cure-all. Laws protect the rare plants from harvest before September. Then, seeds from red berries can be scattered to grow new plants.

Orville's family gathered pine tips to sell by the pound, but at Christmas, pine and hemlock had special uses. Mama and Daddy wrapped wire around evergreen tips to make Christmas wreaths for sale.

As Daddy cut wood for the winter, he cut old cherry trees, not young ones. Mr. Wilcox had a big market for wild cherry bark to be used in cough medicines. Bark from young trees was more valuable, but Daddy couldn't bear to waste the smaller trees for so little wood. After cutting the tree and bringing it home, he cut or peeled the valuable bark away from the wood and sold the bark. He burned the cherry wood for heat.

"We didn't waste nothing," Orville says.

Because galax grew abundantly, it was easy to find and pick. Thus, galax was the most profitable leaf to gather. Per pound, ginseng root was the most valuable herb, though it was rarer than galax. Mama would dig ginseng plants and replant them in her hidden ginseng patch. No one knew where her ginseng was, so it was lost when she died.

In the early fall, Orville collected ragweed pollen. He shook countless ragweed tips before he could fill a little bottle with yellow dust. Mr. Wilcox would pay him two dollars for the bottle of ragweed pollen. Wilcox Drug Company sold Orville's pollen to another company that made allergy medicines.

The Hickses sold most of the herbs they gathered, but Mama kept some for remedies. She brewed sassafras and pennyroyal into soothing teas, and she kept sour blackberry juice in the cellar to use as an antidote for an upset stomach.

Herbs gave Orville's family income and healing, and herbs brought them together. From childhood days of wildcrafting across the mountain, Orville gathered memories along with herbal lore.

62   Witch hazel, also known as beadwood

SHELLING BEANS, BUNCHING GALAX, AND STORYTELLING

That was story time.
—Orville

"Sometimes us young'uns would be out playing in the yard. Mama'd call out, 'You young'uns want to hear a tale?' and we'd come running. She'd show up with a big old tub of beans or a big old tub of peas or a sack of galax."

Mama and the children sat on the porch or in the sitting room. They shelled beans and peas, snapped beans, or bunched galax. When the sun set early, they sat around an oil lamp in the sitting room as they tied galax bunches.

When they bunched galax, the children counted leaf stems and stacked the round leaves neatly—twenty-five for a bunch, forty bunches to a batch of a thousand. Mama cut a big square from a hemp sack and set it across her knee. As the others handed her their bunches of galax, Mama unraveled a string from the hemp square. She placed the galax between her knees, wound the string around the stems, and tied it. Some folks used a galax stem to tie the bunch, but Mama's string was more secure. As she and the children worked, Mama told her stories.

Sometimes when Daddy returned home late after a day's work, the galax would already be tied, the peas shelled, and the stories told. On other evenings, Orville and his family would meet on the porch to work with the day's gatherings. As they worked, Mama and Daddy might talk, but mostly this was story time.

When the galax was all tied and the last story finished, Daddy would say, "Scoot off to bed, young'uns."

Mama dried some of the herbs—life plant and witch hazel. Witch hazel was more valuable dried, though it could be sold fresh.

Sometimes Mama dried her leaves on the wrap-around porch, which protected the plants from the weather. Other times she put the herbs in the attic or on top of the dust building. The dust building was built on a slope, so the tin roof could be reached by walking right off the hill behind it. Mama often dried log moss and witch hazel leaves on the roof.

"Sometimes she put log moss around the edge and leaves in the middle. We'd have to stir them about every hour so they'd dry."

While Mama and the children prepared herbs and produce for sale or use, Orville gathered the stories Mama told—stories full of freshness and ripe for plucking.

Orville picks up a layer of log moss that has grown on a fallen tree.

MAMA'S SONGS AND STORIES

Gallymander, gallymander,
all my gold and silver's gone
and my greaaat long leather purse.
—From "Gallymander," as told by Sarah Hicks

Gold Hicks saw no value in the tales Sarah told her children. "That's a bunch of foolishness," Daddy'd say. Still, he didn't hinder her storytelling.

Mama sang ballads and told stories as she hoed the rows of corn in the garden. Orville would work fast, trying to stay close enough to hear her. Mama knew Orville was trying to keep up, and she used her stories and songs to encourage him to work.

After the day's work was done, Mama would sit on the porch and sing as she strummed her banjo. She sang sad ballads, such as "Pretty Polly" and "The Brown Girl." She sang about John Henry, the legendary railroad builder, and about Tom Dula, who was hung for killing his lover in nearby Wilkes County. (The Kingston Trio recorded a Beech Mountain version of "Tom Dooley," using lines first sung by Orville's cousin, Frank Proffitt, Sr.) Mama sang gospel songs and also folksongs, such as "Lazy John" and "Grandma's Rocking Chair."

Mama had a broad repertoire of stories too. She told a number of traditional tales. "Gallymander," a tale of stolen coins, was her favorite. Mama'd say, "Has anybody seen a little girl with a jig and a jag and a long leather bag?" She told "Catskin," which Orville describes as "sort of a Cinderella story."

Mama also told Jack Tales. "She told 'Old Fire Dragon,' 'Big Jack and Little Jack,' 'Soldier Jack,' and 'Jack and the Robbers,'" says Orville. For Orville, the stories offered can-do messages as the underdog Jack outwitted kings, beasts, tricksters, and crafty brothers.

Mama told ghost tales as well. She told local stories about Old Tough Road and also traditional tales, such as "I Want My Big Toe" and "Sop, Doll, Sop."

Mama's stories were not just sources of laughter; they were also teaching tales. "Soap, Soap, Soap" helped the children remember what they were sent to buy at the store. In the story, as a boy walks to a store to buy soap, he repeats the reminder, "Soap, soap, soap."

"Mama told stories for entertainment," Orville says. With few books except the Bible in his home, with no TV, and without seeing a movie until he was twelve years old, Orville's life was filled with stories.

Stories and Kinfolk

We may have heard the tale a thousand times,
but we couldn't wait to hear it again.
—Orville

Orville's relatives around Beech Mountain shared their tales often. While some stories were well-known, each teller added a signature twist to the tale. Cousin Ray Hicks told "Jack and the Heifer's Hide," "Jack's Hunting Trip," "Jack and the Doctor's Girl," and more.

Uncle Adie Harmon, Mama's brother, told "Old Fire Dragon," "Jack and the Heifer's Hide," and others. He also sang traditional songs and played the banjo. When the children visited him at his home in nearby Matney, he got them to help him chop wood and carry water. He often started telling a tale, captured their interest with the story, and then stopped with the tale half told.

"Come back and work some more next week for me, and I'll tell you the rest of the tale," he'd say.

Orville and the other children were eager to return.

Storytelling held a familiar place in family visits. Orville remembers gathering for stories on a porch or around a fire or wood stove. He joined cousins Ted and Leonard at Ray and Rosa's home as Ray masterfully led them through adventures with Jack. He sat beside cousin Bennie on Uncle Adie's porch as Adie spun tales.

From each teller of tales, Orville learned colorful expressions, theatrical skills, and clever versions of their lively mountain stories.

Uncle Adie Harmon, Mama's brother

Orville's older brother John near where Orville's daddy and brothers built the bus house

Orville traveled up and down the road that wound around Valle Mountain between Valle Crucis and Matney.

68

SCHOOL

Mama'd get us up about six o'clock to get us ready for school.
She'd make sure we washed our faces. If she didn't walk with us to
the bus house, she'd watch us till we got to the gate.
—Orville

Orville attended school at Valle Crucis, about five miles away. During his first year of school there, Orville was in a one-room schoolhouse. "We got milk in glass bottles back then," Orville says. Afterwards, he was in "the big school," a stone building that still stands at the school in Valle Crucis.

Sometime after he started school, his daddy and brothers built a "bus house" to shelter the children as they waited for the bus. To reach the bus house a half mile away, they had to cross the mountain by way of Russell Farthing's land, where his big bull roamed and frightened the children. Mama often walked with them to and from the bus house to be sure they were safe.

"One time we caught a polecat on the way to school," says Orville. "I was about eight or nine years old."

Orville, Mary, and Jerry were walking through the woods to the bus stop. Ronnie, Monty, and Sylvester, sons of their oldest brother Hassell, walked with them. When the children saw the skunk, the boys ran after it. The frightened skunk ran under an overhanging rock, but one of the boys grabbed it from behind. All received the effect of the skunk's spray, including Mary.

"I don't know why the driver let us on the bus," Orville says with a chuckle. "When we got to school, the principal sent us right back home. He said, 'Don't come back until that smell is gone!'"

In school at Valle Crucis, Orville found himself in a world that expected children to grasp lessons easily. Orville did not. The fit was painful.

"I didn't learn nothing," Orville says. He did learn to add and subtract, but division didn't make sense. When he didn't understand the work, he couldn't do the homework. His teachers were not tolerant. "I was always in trouble," he says. "I got a lot of whippings for not doing my homework."

Besides, school brought him face-to-face with students who thought they were better than he was and who teased him for his mountain ways and speech.

As the youngest child, many of Orville's clothes were hand-me-downs. Others came from a used clothing store in Norwood Hollow near Banner Elk. Occasionally, the children got something new from Mast Store.

"One time Mama made us shirts out of flour sacks. Some of the more [well] to-do kids would make fun of us," says Orville.

"We had to walk a long ways to get to school. We'd get muddy sometimes. One time I dropped my books in a mud hole, and I had to pay for them.

"I hated being in school, hated being in class, being shut up."

"Back then, people used to bring food to the school—tomatoes and other food from their gardens," Orville says. The food was prepared for students' lunches.

The school also grew potatoes for lunches. Students helped plant the potatoes in the spring, and the custodian tended them until harvest time. Orville knew about planting potatoes, tending them, and harvesting them. He had planted and dug many potatoes before. From fourth grade until eighth grade, he volunteered to help dig the potatoes in the fall.

"I was tickled to get out of class," he says.

"We couldn't afford to eat in school. For a long time we took our lunch. Usually we had a biscuit and some peanut butter on it. I felt funny sitting in the lunch room with the others eating hot meals. Finally, they must have felt sorry for us and let us eat too."

Even taking lunch money to school later had its problems. "On the bus, some bigger boy stuck a knife up to me and took my lunch money," Orville says.

For several days, Orville was taunted by the boy, but then Mama got word of what was happening. She met the bus with words for the bully. Then she turned to the bus driver, saying, "You'd better keep an eye on my young'uns or I'm not going to send them to school no more!"

One facet of school caught Orville's interest, though—the stories. After reading "The Three Sneezes" at school, Orville decided to make the story his own. He told it to his cousin Ray but added Jack as the character in the story.

"Gaw," Ray said, "you can remember things like that?"

"I learned a cowboy song too. Anything like that I was interested in, I could remember—about cowboys or the woods," Orville recalls.

Orville read about pioneer life in Laura Ingalls Wilder's books, *Little House in the Big Woods* and *Little House on the Prairie*. "I liked *Little House in the Big Woods* so much that I memorized part of it. I was in fourth grade. My teacher let me read three or four pages to the class."

When Orville finished reading, the teacher praised his reading.

Orville had always felt the power of story in Mama's voice, and now he gathered his own seeds of power as he read books from school.

BOY OF THE WOODS

Some people can walk through the woods and not see much.
It's there, though. Being in the woods keeps your mind open.
—Ted Hicks

Orville's best memory of school is that of not going. He claims that, while in fourth grade, he went to school only two or three times one month. On the other days, he hid in the woods when the school bus was coming.

While Orville found school an uncomfortable fit, he was at home in the woods, where he could hunt or gather herbs. He was content to be alone there. By the time he was nine, he often chose to go to the woods instead of to school.

"It's so pretty in the woods," he says, reflecting on his refuge from school. "Mama gave us lunch money, but I wouldn't need it in the woods. I gave it to Mary and Jerry. I told them I wasn't going to school and told them not to tell Mama and Daddy."

They didn't tell.

Orville left Mary and Jerry before they got on the bus. He headed to Laurel Creek or to Dead-a-lock. The hollow there had few of the valuable herbs that Mama collected. Neither she nor Daddy would have reason to wander there and find their son skipping school.

When school officials asked Orville where he had been, he said, "I've been helping Mama and Daddy on the farm." On fair weather days, the teacher accepted the excuse. When weather was bad, he knew the teacher would doubt that explanation of his absence. He went to school on those days.

Some days when Orville stayed out of school, he walked across Beech Mountain to Ray and Rosa's home. "Ray would see me coming and say, 'Ain't you supposed to be in school?' and I'd say, 'Yeah, but I cut out.' Ray would say, 'Well I won't tell.'"

Orville would spend his day following Ray—talking, listening, working in Ray's potato field.

But Orville spent most of those days alone beneath the trees deep in the woods. There he was free to be himself; there he thrived. At first he sat on the rocks. He was content just to sit for three or four hours. Sometimes he walked or swung on grapevines.

Before long, Orville built a shelter of supple wood. He broke saplings and branches, bent them over, and poked them into the ground to secure them. He left an opening in the front and also at the back of the shelter. Orville covered the top of the shelter with leaves, which kept him dry when rain fell.

Orville carried a fish hook and string in his pocket when he went into the woods. He cut a birch pole. Birch bends but doesn't break easily. He fastened the hook to the string and the string to the pole. Then Orville was ready to fish for trout in Laurel Creek. "That's where the big fishing holes were," he says.

Orville built a fire with matches he had slipped into his pocket before leaving home. To cook his catch for lunch, he speared the fish on a stick and roasted it over the fire. He picked berries and currants to eat.

Sometimes Orville took food from the cellar—canned food or "taters" to roast. "But then Daddy thought someone was stealing his food, so he put a lock on it," Orville says with a chuckle.

Once Orville cut a chunk of meat off the ham Daddy had hung in the smoke house for winter use. When Daddy noticed that a piece of ham was missing, he assumed some varmint had been feasting on the family's food.

"He threw away the whole ham," Orville says.

Orville also caught "lizards," or salamanders, in the woods. Salamanders could be sold for bait. In the afternoon after returning home, he would do his chores and then announce that he was going out to hunt lizards. Instead, he would go back to the peaceful woods and get the salamanders he had already gathered.

In the afternoon, Orville listened for the school bus. He headed home from the woods just in time to walk up the dirt road and through the gate with Mary and Jerry. His parents assumed he had gone to school.

Usually Orville went to the woods alone, but sometimes his nephews Ronnie, Sylvester, and Monty joined him. Their father caught them in the act, though, which ended the nephews' school days in the woods. Still, they didn't tell about Orville's hideout or about the time he spent in the woods.

When Orville's brother Charlie moved back to the mountain from Siler City, he installed a phone. One day when Orville had skipped school, the principal called Charlie to check on Orville. Daddy got word of the call and of Orville's absence from school. Orville remembers the day.

"When I came home, Daddy asked me, 'Where've you been?' I said, 'At school,' and he said, 'No, you ain't.'" That call and "a real good whipping from Daddy" ended Orville's escapes from school and his days in the woods. But for about five years—until he was fourteen years old—the woods offered Orville a haven on many school days.

Orville had learned his practical lessons well. He learned from the wisdom of ancestors who had survived by adapting to the North Carolina mountains. He knew how to find food, how to hunt. He knew how to make a shelter, how to cook over a fire. He knew the plants and trees. He knew which wood bent, which wood was strong.

"You can chew on birch," Orville says. "It's like a toothbrush."

Orville, the shy boy of the woods, gained an intimate knowledge of the natural world, a knowledge that would someday fill his stories.

As Orville hunted in earlier years, he often stopped atop
Rocky Face to sit and look out across the mountains.

HUNTING

*I'd call my little dog Brownie up, put my gun on my shoulder,
and off I'd go across the mountain.*
—Orville

Orville sometimes worked on Frank Baird's farm in Valle Crucis. "I put up hay, cleaned out the barn, set out tobacco," Orville says. Other times, he cut cabbage for Russell Farthing. Orville earned fifty cents per hour for farm work. "I took the money and bought shotgun shells for hunting, and I gave Mama and Daddy a little of it," he says.

When Orville was ten, Daddy took him hunting. Daddy taught his sons to use a gun safely. For them, the gun was not a toy, but rather a tool that enabled them to put meat on the table. By age twelve, Orville was hunting on his own.

Mornings came early. Orville often was hunting in the woods by six o'clock. Having taken some food with him, he could walk through the hills all day. Sometimes he walked to the other side of the mountain, to Rocky Face, or to Hickory Patch. Late in the day, he would return with four or five squirrels and perhaps a grouse.

Some mountain folks call a grouse a "pheasant," but Orville makes a distinction between the long-tailed pheasant and the flat-tailed grouse.

"A pheasant has to run to take off. A grouse can fly right off the ground." The sudden loud beating of a rising grouse's wings is familiar to Orville. "A lot of them wouldn't move till you run up on them. It'd scare you when they'd fly right up in your face.

"One time we were picking strawberries with Mama, and we runned up on a grouse. She had some littl'uns. Mama called them 'diddles.' She'd say, 'Look at them little diddles run!' The littl'uns run this way and that way, and the mama grouse went off with her wing bent like it was broke.

"Another time I was hunting with my brother, and one flew up in front of me. I shot and my brother said, 'Did you get it?' I said 'No, but I shot where it was.'

"If you come home with a grouse, you was proud. You'd really done something."

Snow didn't stop Orville from hunting. "I was out chasing a grouse in the snow," says Orville, "and I got down under the laurel bushes following it till I couldn't find the track. Then I looked up, and there it sat on a limb above me. I was kinda' down on my knees dragging my gun, and I couldn't get my gun up fast enough before it flew off."

Orville is sure the bird got the last laugh.

Orville spent many a snowy day hunting rabbits. "There'd be six or seven of us together—my brothers Charlie and John, Jerry and Willis; my cousin Bennie, sometimes Daddy. We'd be out all day and come back in with about twenty rabbits and a grouse," Orville says.

"A lot of times we'd have rabbit for Thanksgiving. Especially around Thanksgiving or Christmas, Boyd would go rabbit-hunting with me."

Boyd Presnell, son of Orville's sister Frances, lived on a dairy farm near Hickory. "Sometimes in the summer, he'd come up and stay with us for a week or two. Then I'd go down and stay with them on the dairy farm."

Orville trapped rabbits in a wooden box like this.

Orville with his brother-in-law Junior Presnell

Orville's own hunting experience gives a ring of authenticity to his stories. He tells a tale about his uncle's little rabbit dog:

> I had an uncle, lived way back in the mountains. He was out one day with his mowin' scythe, mowin' 'round the house there. I guess it was about dinnertime. His wife hollered at him, "Dinnertime," and he just laid the mowin' scythe up against the fence there—old blade sticking up in the air there. Went in the house to eat dinner.
>
> The little dog was chasin' a rabbit runnin' around there. It chased the rabbit through the back yard and around. Rabbit went under the fence and the little dog went under the fence and hit that mowing scythe blade 'n split himself right in two.
>
> That man heard it, and he runned out and seen that little dog. He grabbed his coat and runned out there and grabbed his little dog and slapped it together. Wrapped it up in his coat and carried it to the house. Put it by the fireplace. He'd go out, and sometimes he'd put a little turpentine down in there.
>
> About a week went by, he heard something. "Hmmmm, hmmmm."
>
> "Oh," he said, "My little dog's alive." He unwrapped that coat, and sure enough, the dog was alive. Got to lookin', he'd slapped him upside down—two legs up and two legs down.
>
> The little dog lived and done good. They was so glad. It was a sight. They'd see it run a rabbit. Said he didn't know how—little dog'd run on two legs. If he got tired he'd jump and turn over and run on the other two legs. He said a rabbit hardly ever got away from it. He said it was the only dog in the mountains that could bark out of both ends.

Mama's Squirrel Stew

We'd stand around with a spoon in our hands till it got done.
—Orville

Skin three or four squirrels. Cut the legs and head off, and cut the squirrels into several pieces. Put them in a big pot. Let it boil. Cut up 'taters in it and an onion head. Maybe put a little corn in it or peas and a carrot—whatever's on hand. Let it boil a long time, and then let it simmer. Sprinkle a little flour in it and simmer till it gets thick. Season it with salt and pepper.

Daddy wove this chair seat of white oak strips around 1940.

FROM THE TREES

Manuel looked like a haystack, he had so many baskets on him.
—Orville, describing his grandfather on the way to sell his baskets

"Daddy and my grandfather Manual Hicks made a lot of baskets," Orville says. "Daddy's brother Luther did too.

"I used to watch Daddy. It took a long time to get ready to make a basket."

Orville describes Daddy's simple basket-making tool, a steel plate with five holes in decreasing sizes. Daddy fastened the metal piece to the woodshed, where he prepared wood strips for weaving.

"Daddy mostly used white oak. It would bend. Sometimes he used ash. Daddy'd split a strip off a white oak log—about half the size of your finger. He took a pocket knife and hewed it down. Then he pulled it through the first hole. The next hole was smaller, and he pulled the strip through that one. By the time he got it through the fifth hole, it was pretty smooth and round—about the round of a pencil."

Daddy's baskets, woven from these wood strips, were handy on the farm. "Mama'd go to the cellar with a basket and carry five or six cans of food back to the house in it," Orville says. "After Daddy cut wood, I picked up chips in a basket." The chips would kindle a fire. "I picked many a berry into one too—and gathered eggs."

"Manuel made a lot of baskets too. He carried twenty-five or thirty baskets to the store to trade for whatever he could get—flour, sugar, or money. He'd have so many baskets on him, you could hardly see him."

Daddy used white oak strips to make chair bottoms too. "When Daddy made a chair bottom, it lasted. We've still got a chair with a bottom he made. I expect Daddy made it around 1940."

Daddy also crafted sleds from the wood he cut. He made one- and two-horse sleds that he used in the garden and as he gathered wood.

"Daddy'd get the bottom of an oak or ash where it curved like a runner. He'd cut the runners and lay them in the water in the spring box.

"I liked to watch him make sleds. Those big sleds took four or five people to move. I'd give anything to have one of his sleds now."

But the sleds are gone with time.

As Daddy made sleds, he pounded pegs into the wood with a knot maul. "He probably had that maul since the 1940s," Orville says. "He took a big old knot out of a tree, cut it down to round it, and put a handle in it. It was so hard you couldn't bust it."

"One time Daddy made a bow for us. He got it hewed out and laid it in the spring box. He let it sit there in the water all winter.

"When it was finished, it was really smooth and pretty. It was as good as any bow you'd buy in a store."

The boys made their own arrows from reeds that grew nearby. "We'd put a piece of paper in the end to make it shoot straight. If you didn't put that paper in, then it'd go every which a-way. I learned to shoot pretty good with it.

"Daddy was good at making things. If he set his mind to it, he could make anything."

While Daddy could craft just about anything out of wood, Orville turned his craftiness to stories.

Daddy's knot maul, made in the 1940s, is now at the Appalachian Cultural Museum.

Orville made a miniature sled like the horse-drawn farm sleds his father made.

Orville and his sister
Mary at Fort Bragg

Orville and Sylvia soon
after they were married
in 1972

Part III.

Adult Years

Sylvia

If I had the wings of a beautiful dove,
I'd fly away to the girl I love,
which would be you, Sis.
—Orville, written to Sylvia before their marriage

Orville left home and entered the Army when he was eighteen years old. After basic training at Fort Bragg, he spent time at Fort Benning, Georgia, and Fort Polk, Louisiana. The Army took Orville to parts of the country he had never seen, but he longed to return to the mountains.

Orville was twenty when he met Sylvia Huffman. Sylvia, often called Sis, was sixteen. His sister Hattie's husband, Bennie Presnell, sang with the Presnell Quartet. Orville went to hear Bennie sing at Shady Grove Baptist Church in Morganton. He met Sylvia there.

"I was so good looking she couldn't resist me," Orville says with a grin.

Sylvia adds, "I think it worked both ways."

For a short while, they "courted up and down the road," but not for long. They married four months later, in 1972, on Orville's twenty-first birthday—"so I'll be sure to remember my anniversary," he says. Within six months, they were expecting their first child.

During their early years of marriage, Sylvia and Orville often gathered herbs—galax, moss, beadwood, and others. They cut pine tips and made wreaths to sell.

Sylvia remembers the feel of rough beadwood twigs as she ran her hand across them to pull off leaves. "Sometimes your hands would get real raw and sore," she says.

"After pulling leaves for so long, then you would just get used to it," says Orville.

As Orville's mother had done, Sylvia canned in abundance to prepare for cold winters. She learned to prepare for lean times and for times when weather kept her family inside.

Sylvia had stocked her pantry before the blizzard of 1993. When a relief helicopter dropped food, she and Orville shared what they received. "We didn't need it," Sylvia said.

Orville and Sylvia spent two years in Burke County, where Orville worked for Burke Yarns, but indoor work did not suit his nature. They moved back to the mountains—back to where Orville's roots ran deep, back to where his stories were rooted.

Orville's brother Willis

The family: Sarah and Gold Hicks in front of their family: (left to right) Orville, Jerry, Charlie, Nancy, Hassell, Frances, and Hattie

A Farewell to the Homeplace

I'd like to go back and see it again.
—Orville, reflecting on his homeplace

In 1976, Orville's homeplace burned. His parents barely got out in time. Orville, Sylvia, and their sons Orville, Jr., and Wayne were living upstairs at the time. Wayne was a newborn. They were away from home when the fire started— Orville at Ray's home, Sylvia and the boys with her mother in Morganton.

The fire destroyed not only the wooden house but also possessions and family history in pictures. "We lost everything we had," Orville says, "pictures, memories, Bobby's things." Orville's brother Bobby had died in a car accident at age nineteen.

Sylvia had been honored with a baby shower for Wayne. The gifts were lost in the fire—diapers included.

Until a replacement could be built, Mama and Daddy lived in a room over the cellar. Orville and Sylvia moved into the one-room corn crib near the house. One day, Daddy came into the corn crib and measured the fold-out bed Orville and Sylvia were using. He told Sylvia that he was going to make a bed frame, his contribution to their comfort in the small room Orville and Sylvia called home.

Looking back, Orville doesn't speak of his early life as hard, but Sylvia remembers the time they spent in the corn crib. "Now, that was hard," Sylvia admits.

Members of Bethany Baptist Church helped build a new house just uphill from the first one. Only the old cellar remains from the earlier buildings—and memories.

Yes, memories.

Sylvia and Joe, Christmas 1990

STORYTELLER ON THE HOME FRONT

Orville came here, and Daddy said, "You'll be the one."
—Ted Hicks, recalling Ray's expectations of Orville as a storyteller

For Sarah Hicks, who grew up in an environment that valued stories, storytelling came naturally. The thought of her youngest son as a storyteller in the public eye "never entered her mind," Orville says.

Orville honed his storytelling skills with his own five sons: Orville, Jr., Wayne, Donnie, Curt, and Joe. Each night, he told them two or more tales at bedtime.

"Tell another story, Daddy," they would say as he finished a tale.

"I'd tell another tale, and then I'd be about ready to turn off the light, and one of them would say, 'Daddy, I want to hear another one!'" Orville could have told stories well into the night.

Joe especially enjoyed Orville's personal adaptations of the stories. "Put me doing it," Joe would say, so Orville replaced a character's name with Joe's.

Orville and Sylvia's sons liked to spend the night at Grandma's. As a child, Orville delighted in his mother's stories, and now Sarah Hicks charmed her grandchildren. "They couldn't wait to go to Grandma's and hear her tales," Orville says.

Sarah Hicks's birthday was on Halloween. Orville, Sylvia, and their sons visited her then. The boys dressed up so their grandma couldn't tell who they were. She always gave them some candy.

Sylvia recalls these annual visits. "We would come up on the porch with birthday presents for her. The kids would take off their masks as we started up on the porch, and she would know who it was then. She would always laugh and seem to get a real thrill out of it. And, of course, whatever the gift was, she always said she loved it."

Those nights, Grandma's stories were short because the boys had other stops to make. "We'd go on over the mountain trick-or-treating," says Orville.

As his sons grew, Orville's thoughts often drifted to his earlier days in the woods. One morning, an unexpected event reminded him of his childhood.

Curt and Donnie, then ages nine and eleven, headed down the hill to meet the school bus as usual.

"I picked up a book and was sitting on the couch," Orville says. "Next thing I knew, one boy hit the floor. It scared me. Insulation was falling and Sheetrock. I couldn't see who it was. He was white all over with dust from the Sheetrock. All I could see was his eyes as he ran out the door and down the road. I heard another one still up there in the attic.

"I got to looking and said to Sylvia, 'That's Donnie!' Curt and Donnie had slipped in the back door and gone up in the attic instead of to school. Donnie had stepped on the Sheetrock and fallen through the ceiling.

"They'd heard me talk about staying out of school, and they thought they'd do it too. After all the time I'd gone to the woods instead of school, I couldn't be too hard on them. I told them, 'Come back here, boys. I'm not going to whip you this time, but we'd better get that ceiling fixed before the landlord finds it. And don't do that no more.'" With help from Orville's long-time friend Larry Rominger, they repaired the ceiling in short order.

A new generation of stories was unfolding.

PASSING THE STORYTELLING TORCH

I don't see how Orville did it. I'd be saying,
"Where's the door or where do you want one?"
—Ted Hicks, on Orville's first public storytelling

As Orville had done in his childhood, he later sat in storytelling circles at Ray and Rosa's home. Now his sons joined him.

"They'd sit there and listen and laugh. Their eyes would get that big." Orville measures a circle with his thumb and a finger.

Curt often followed Rosa as she kindled the wood stove and baked biscuits to feed the hungry crowd. Donnie especially liked Ted.

Not only did Ray tell stories in family gatherings, but Orville took his turn too. Ray delighted in Orville's storytelling.

"Gawd!" Ray would say. "You're good." The tales were familiar to Ray, but still, he would get tickled as he heard Orville's yarn-spinning.

"Ray'd be listening to me tell a story," Orville says, "and he'd say, 'Yeah, that's right.' He'd throw his big hands out." Orville stretches his own arms wide, palms up.

Ray would say to Orville, "You can always tell a good storyteller because he can make up a story as he goes along."

As Ray and his biographer, Robert Isbell, sat on the porch talking one day, Orville walked up. "There comes the man who's going to carry the torch when I'm gone," Ray proclaimed.

At the time of Sarah Hicks's death in 1986, Orville had not yet told his first story before an audience. Sarah never knew the legacy that would follow her through Orville, her eleventh child, who had learned her stories over beans, galax, and rows of corn.

Orville started telling stories publicly in late 1986, about half a year after his mother's death. At the time, his youngest son, Joe, was a baby.

Orville went to Ray's home on the day of the Beech Mountain Folktale Festival. "You go on. I'll come in a bit," Orville told the others. But in the quiet of

Orville, the young storyteller, 1987

the old mountain home, his shyness took over, and he lingered there away from the crowd.

Later that day, Ray sent a friend back to the house to fetch Orville. Ray wanted Orville to help tell a ghost story. The invitation to tell a tale came as a surprise. Flattered but unsure, Orville headed to the festival.

That night, with Ray's encouragement, Orville told his first tale before a public audience.

"I know you're gonna be nervous. I was," Ray said. "It's gonna be dark, though. You can't hardly see nobody. They're people just like you are. I know you're good. Just be yourself."

"I was real nervous, but I told the tale," Orville says. In shadows, before listeners who could barely see him, Orville told a ghost tale of a boy who cut off a woolly beast's toe and put it in a pot of beans. At night the beast came looking for his toe. "I want my big toe. I want my big toe," the beast said as it came closer and closer.

In the days that followed, Ray continued to encourage Orville to tell tales. When Orville told stories, he saw smiles on the listeners' faces. Children's eyes lit up, and adults rocked with laughter. Their responses kept him telling stories over and over—each telling fresh as it came to a new audience.

Orville tells stories at the Watauga Public Library in Boone, 1989.

Orville, Ray, and Ray's wife, Rosa, traveled together to storytelling events. Traveling was an adventure for the Beech Mountain trio. They drove to folktale festivals in Jonesboro, Tennessee, and Thurmond, Virginia. They went to the MerleFest Bluegrass Festival in Wilkesboro, North Carolina. They traveled to Kentucky and Georgia. Rosa joined Ray in singing "Barbary Allen," "Leaving on the New River Train," and "The Morning Stars Are Rising." Orville and Ray shared their tales with all who listened.

"The tale belongs to everybody," Ray told Orville.

Orville at MerleFest in North Wilkesboro

Orville and Ray at Maggie Valley

In The Company of a Friend

Study with me now.
—Ray Hicks

Orville grew up going to Ray for haircuts, and for forty years, he continued to do so. "He only had one way to cut," Orville says with his typical mischievous twinkle. "He cut till he ran out of hair."

Once when Orville went to Ray for a haircut, he told Ray to cut a little off here, pointing—then a little there, pointing— and then somewhere else.

"I never cut hair like that before," Ray said with a laugh.

"Well, that's the way you did it last time," Orville said.

Another time, as Ray rode in Orville's car, Ray complained that something in the seat was poking him. "I guess you can just throw it out the window," Orville teased.

After stirring about, Ray announced, "That got it!" He held up the buckle from the seat belt that Orville had just installed. Ray had cut the buckle off the strap.

Orville laughs. "I could never get mad at Ray. He was always so good natured."

During Ray's later years, Orville wrote a song to honor his cousin, friend, story-telling mentor, and "second dad." He called it "The Ballad of Ray Hicks." Using a salvaged guitar, which he adapted from a twelve-string to a six-string instrument ("I didn't know how to play a twelve-string," he explained.), Orville played chords to accompany himself as he sang his ballad for Ray.

Obviously touched by the song, Ray expressed his gratitude. "What makes it so good is that it comes from the heart," the elder Ray told Orville.

In April of 2003, Orville sang "The Ballad of Ray Hicks" at Ray's funeral.

The Ballad of Ray Hicks
Written by Orville Hicks
June 23, 2001

High on the mountain
Where the sun always shines,
There lives a man
Who is tall as the pines.

His hair is turning,
Turning a little gray.
He's the master of the storytellers,
but he's known by his friends as Big Ray.

(Chorus)
No, no, I say
There'll never be another Ray,
For when they made that man,
They throwed that mold away.

You can go to his house.
He will say, "Just come on in."
He's a-sitting in his chair by the fire,
On his face a big ol' grin.

He'll play his harp, tell you a tale,
And he might even sing you a song.
Before you knowed it,
You been up at Ray Hicks's all day long.

(Chorus)
No, no, I'll say
There'll never be another Ray,
For when they made that man,
They throwed that mold away.

There's their son Ted.
He's the youngest boy.
He's always full of laughter,
And his heart is full of joy.

Now there's little Rosa,
Who has the voice of a morning dove.
She gets to singing "Little Black Train A-coming."
You'll think you are in Heaven above.

When I get to feeling
A little lonely or sad,
Why, I just go up to see Ray and Rosa,
My second mom and dad.

(Chorus)
No, no, I say
There'll never be another Ray,
For when they made that man,
They throwed that mold away.

No, no, I'll say
There'll never be another Ray.
I swear, when they made that man,
They throwed that mold away.

Daddy and Mama

Generations Gone

I'd come walking home, and I'd see Mama sitting there on the porch breaking beans. Daddy'd be out cutting wood or mowing on the bank with the mowing scythe.
—Orville

Despite Daddy's earlier scorn of stories, his attitude mellowed with the years. Toward the end of his life, Orville's daddy took more interest in Orville's storytelling. At last, he went to hear Orville tell old tales and spin new ones. While Orville's daddy wasn't one to express pride, his presence at Orville's storytelling performances carried a message.

Orville's father died in 1994.

Neither siblings nor cousins from the Beech Mountain area were actively telling traditional tales beyond the community. With Mama's death in 1986 and Ray's in 2003, the storytelling torch passed to Orville's hands.

Ray and his harmonica

Jack and His Maw, linoleum print by Gail E. Haley,
author and illustrator of *Mountain Jack Tales*

ORVILLE AND JACK

The last time I was down by there to see Jack,
that lazy rascal still ain't done a good day's work.
—Orville's last words from "Jack and the Varmints"

Orville laughs at the fact that he now goes to school to tell his stories. The mountain speech of his upbringing, once a subject of taunting at school, now serves him well as it gives color and authenticity to the tales he tells.

The love of stories Orville learned from his mother remains with him. His knowledge of a life that depends on crops, firewood, and a balance between man and nature prepares him for telling tales of the mountain boy Jack. While Orville learned the stories of earlier generations, experience offers fodder for new and adapted tales.

As Orville says, "Anybody can be Jack," and most of us will identify at some point with this wily underdog of the folktales.

"I'm kind of a Jack," says Orville, that familiar twinkle slipping into his eyes.

Orville's life on the mountain gives him an understanding of Jack's circumstances. In the Jack Tales Orville heard from childhood, Jack grows up in the mountains. Often, his mama is nearly out of food, and Jack is looking for work. Jack trades to get what he needs. "That's kinda' how we growed up," Orville says.

"Jack is always going out over the mountain, going out to cut firewood." Orville grew up doing these same chores. Jack scrounges to make ends meet. Orville faced that challenge too. He says, "Sometimes I'd think, 'Now, what would Jack do?'"

Orville grew up with older brothers who sometimes played tricks on him. In the tales, Tom and Will often try to get the best of Jack. Somehow, in spite of their efforts, Jack always gets the best of his crafty brothers.

Not only did Jack encounter mischief his brothers handed him, but he also dealt with looming threats. Growing up on the mountain, Orville had seen larger-than-life threats: darkness, blizzards, and wild animals. Jack's success offered a heartening message.

"I tell a tale called 'Jack and the Devil,'" Orville says. He begins:

Jack was out one day walkin' and he met up with the devil. The old devil and Jack got to talkin', and the devil said, "Jack, let's me and you go in together and do somethin'."

Jack said, "What do you want to do?"

Devil said, "I don't know."

Jack said, "Well, let's raise some 'taters."

That devil said, "That sounds good to me. How would we divide 'em?"

Jack said, "Well, I'll just take what grows under the ground and you can have what grows on top of the ground."

Devil shook his hand and said, "You got a deal."

Well, it come harvesting time. Jack went out there and dug all them pretty 'taters out from under the ground—big old round 'taters, a paper sack full of 'em. Devil, all he got was the tops. He took 'em down there and they wasn't worth nothin'.

Boy, he got mad, and he come back. He said, "Jack, let's raise something else together."

Jack said, "How 'bout corn?"

"Yeah, Jack, that sounds good to me." But he said, "This time you take what grows on top of the ground and let me have what grows under the ground."

Jack said, "You got a deal."

Well, it come time to harvest that corn. Jack got all them roastin' ears out of the top of that corn, and all the devil got was a bunch of roots you pull out of the ground. He ended up with nothin' again. Boy, he was gettin' madder and madder.

He said, "Jack, let's do something else."

Jack said, "Let's raise some hogs."

Devil said, "Well, I can't go wrong with that. Let's give it a try."

They raised two hundred hogs. Well, they got bigger enough to divide. They was going there one morning to divide them. And Jack had put him a fence on the left-hand side of the hog pen, and the devil got one on the right-hand side. Well, Jack cut a hole in his little fence to the devil's fence and put corn out there in his fence. Every time the devil'd pick up a hog 'n put it in his side, it'd run over to the fence and run out there where all Jack's hogs were eatin' that corn.

They got done dividing them two hundred hogs. Devil looked over, and he didn't have a one in his fence. Looked over in Jack's side, and there was all them big hogs out there.

Devil said, "Which ones is mine?"

Jack said, "I don't know, but I twisted all mine's tails before I throwed them in my side of the fence."

Devil looked over, and all two hundred hogs had twisted tails. He couldn't tell which ones were his, so he ended up with nothin' again.

Old devil never could get the best of Jack.

A Storyteller, Indeed

He lifts people up.
—Ted Hicks, on his cousin Orville

"I used to get whipped for telling lies. Now I get paid for it. I never thought I'd be traveling and doing this storytelling for a living," Orville says.

While none of Orville's family members have joined him in telling tales, they have supported him. Orville shares part-time work with his son Curt at the Aho Recycling Center in Watauga County. When Orville has storytelling opportunities, Curt covers the recycling job. Orville's youngest son, Joe, was only fourteen when he set up Orville's web page. While Wayne hasn't followed his father in storytelling, he has written some songs that have made appearances in Nashville.

"I keep up with things," Sylvia says. She handles the bookings, business, and e-mail. Orville would rather not fiddle with computers.

As Orville tells stories at the Greensboro Historical Museum, Sylvia sells tapes, CDs and books.

Orville admits feeling nervous before telling tales, but after he gets started, he relaxes and enjoys his role. When Orville tells stories at a university or at the National Mall in Washington, D.C., he begins with a casual greeting and the same neighborly tone he would use in a school or in the cozy setting of the Todd General Store near his home. His tales hold listeners of all ages spellbound.

Through the years, Ray told tales with his eyes right on Orville. Now Orville follows that example when he tells stories. "I pick me out two or three people to look at and talk to," says Orville, "no matter how many people are there. When I made that CD over in Boone, they put me in a little room by myself to tell stories. There was a fly on the wall, so I just told to it." The memory brings out a familiar laugh.

"I think the younger generation needs to know how folks lived here in the mountains." He especially likes "to see the kids' faces," to see their delight in the twists and turns of his stories.

"I like telling stories, but I don't like the travel," Orville says. He'll choose his own bed any day over a fancy room at the prestigious Grove Park Inn in Asheville, and he prefers Sylvia's cooking to a meal in a crowded restaurant. In June of 2003, a trip to the Smithsonian Folk Life Festival in Washington, D.C., allowed him to tell stories on the National Mall alongside cousin Frank Proffitt, Jr., who sang ballads there. Orville was grateful for the experience but glad to plant his feet back on the familiar soil of Watauga County, North Carolina.

Orville and Sylvia, the day he received the Paul Green Multi-media Award

Orville laughs as he tells stories at Todd General Store, 2004.

Orville still gets tickled and laughs out loud as he tells his stories. "I just like them," he explains. "I always loved stories. I couldn't wait to hear them."

Once a traveler told Orville, "If I could bottle that laughter and take it back to Florida to sell, I'd be rich."

Sylvia sees the freshness of Orville's stories. Though she knows them by heart, she still laughs too—often ahead of the story.

Orville knows that laughter is good medicine, and so he tells his tales. He simply picks his stories as he goes along, letting one story flow into another as only a master storyteller could. "I ain't never in my life sat down and planned what stories I was going to tell."

"How many Jack Tales do you know?" a listener asked Orville after hearing some tales.

Orville answered, "A sackful."

Mama stocked her cellar with potatoes and jars of beans, but Orville kept a stock of stories. With his harvest of tales at hand, Orville fits his stories to the situation.

6TH

JACK TAL
Rememb

Bring
Chairs

THE
GASTON COUNTY PUBLIC LIBRA
And
FRIENDS of the GASTON COUNTY PUB
Proudly Present
Award-Winning Storyteller

ORVILLE H
In
MOUN
TWISTS
Appalachian S

MerleFest '96
ARTIST
Orville Hicks
Ray & Orville Hicks

ORVILLE
HICKS
WOODBERRY FOREST

Orville
Orville Hicks
Storyteller
High Country, NC

THE NORTH CAROLINA FOLKLORE SOCIETY

NCSE
North Carolina Society of Engineers

ORVILLE
HICKS
Our State
North Carolina

FIREFLY FOLK FESTIVAL
BOONE, NC. 866
ADULT

ORVILLE HICKS STORYTELLER

...from the renowned Hicks
of Watauga County...
Jack Tales
for all ages

...unusually
wonderful...

SUNDAY, MY
3:00 P.M.
CELO INN
TICKETS $4 at door
$2.50 in advance
seating limited

25

In 1995 at the opening of North Carolina Museum of History in Raleigh, Orville told the story of the mule eggs to an audience that included Governor Jim Hunt. In the story, Orville poses as a crafty mountain boy who sells pumpkins. A gullible city slicker buys not only a pumpkin but also the boy's pitch that the pumpkins are mule eggs. As he told the story, Orville pointed to the governor and suggested that he looked a little like the city slicker. Later, the two men laughed together over Orville's spur-of-moment twist in his tale.

"Hey, Mr. Hicks, have you got any of those mule eggs with you?" Governor Hunt teased.

Once as he told the story of Hardy Hardhead at a school, he left out one of the seven characters. A little boy who knew the story spoke up, reminding him of the omission. Orville just put his finger to his lips. "Shh," he said softly. "He's a secret." Then he continued with the story, weaving the character into the plot at a critical moment—to the delight of the boy and the other children.

Time has brought change to the Beech Mountain area. With Ray's death, family story-swapping happens less frequently. Still, Orville and Ray's son Ted swap a few tales. With his own sons grown, Orville still finds a listener in his teen-age granddaughter, Jenny Lynn, daughter of Orville, Jr., and his wife, Christie.

"One day she called me and said 'Guess what, Grandpa! We've got show and tell at school, and I nominated you to come down and tell stories.'" So Orville went to school and told "Fill, Bowl, Fill," Jenny Lynn's favorite tale.

Orville hopes that someday his granddaughter will join him on the storytelling stage.

"It'd be a shame if no one took up these tales," Orville says.

Buttons, badges, and fliers: storytelling mementos.

The Gut Bucket

A lot of people on the mountain made them.
My brother made them. Everyone made them a little different.
—Orville

During Orville's growing years, his daddy allowed the family to listen to the Grand Ole Opry on a battery-powered radio. "We couldn't tap our toes, though. Daddy thought it was sinful if we tapped our toes to music, and he'd turn off the radio." Orville especially enjoyed the blue grass music of Bill Monroe.

Folks on the mountain made their own music too. Even Orville's daddy played the guitar as he sang gospel music. The banjo and the dulcimer have held prominent places in the music around Beech Mountain. Several of Orville's kinfolk made these instruments.

When instruments were not available, folks on the mountain improvised. Orville shows his miniature version of the gut bucket, so named for the materials used to make it.

"Folks couldn't afford a string bass," Orville says, "so they made these gut buckets, or washtub basses, as some people call them." Orville plucks the single string. In years past, the string would have been gut, or sinew.

"I had a great old big one at work. It was made out of a washtub." Orville explains that the instrument was often made from a washtub or a bucket, hence the familiar name, washtub bass.

"I made this from things I salvaged at work," he says. His small version is made from a large coffee can. A string from discarded mini-blinds connects the bottom of the inverted can to a horizontal handle. The handle is fastened on top of a pole that rises beside the bucket. "That was an old hoe handle," he says, smiling.

Orville's washtub bass or gut bucket

"You can move the handle and change the sound, or you can put a different string on it and make the sound different." Orville skillfully presses the handle to adjust the tension. He strokes the string with his finger and sings his version of "Black Jack Davy."

Black Jack Davy came
a-riding through the woods,
singing so loud and gaily.
Many green trees around him stood,
and he charmed the hearts of the ladies.

"How old are you, my pretty little miss?
How old are you my lady?"
She replied with a "Hee, hee, hey,
I'll be sixteen next Sunday."

THE BANJO

Council Harmon'd hear a banjo
and he couldn't help dancing.
—Orville

On a warm June day, Orville sits atop a cellar built against a bank by his home. In the shade of nearby trees, he strums an old banjo. Birds sing along in a mix of melodies.

"A feller give me this banjo and these dulcimers. He said he was pretty sure some of my people made the banjo and that big dulcimer. The other one came from Kentucky. A lot of my people made these—Stanley Hicks; Ray's daddy, Nathan Hicks; Tab Ward and others." Orville's brother Hassell made several banjos and sang as well.

Orville knows a treasure when he sees one.

"This one here's a fretless banjo," says Orville. "See, that dulcimer has frets." He points to the ridges that mark the frets on the dulcimer. The banjo is handcrafted of maple and held together with pegs. "This is real groundhog hide on it." He shows the head on the resonator box. The skin is smooth on the outside but textured on the inside.

Orville strums and sings song after song.

Going up Cripple Creek all in a whirl,
Going up Cripple Creek to see my girl.

Orville strums an old handcrafted banjo.
A dulcimer sits on the bench in front of him.

"Yeah, I think I'll see about getting this banjo fixed up with new strings," he says with a nod. Wooden tuning pegs hold the strings over the neck of the banjo. "A banjo with wooden pegs like this is hard to keep tuned. Stanley Hicks used to say wooden pegs were enough to make a preacher cuss."

Orville picks another tune and sings.

"I sure wish I knew who made this thing."

Orville is a collector, a salvager of odds and ends of his family story—in relics, in memories, in words, and in songs.

Stanley Hicks, Orville's cousin and well-known maker of banjos and dulcimers

DRAWING FROM THE HILLS AND HOLLOWS

*Orville has gathered herbs from childhood and into adulthood.
These herbs brought about healing. Similarly, Orville has
spent his life gathering stories in a way that is also healing.*
—Sharon Kimball,
Director of Education at the Appalachian Cultural Museum

Besides storytelling, many of Orville's other interests are rooted in his childhood. After playing softball with a carved bat and a ball made from a tin can and rubber strips, Orville later spent twenty years pitching for softball teams in Boone and Matney. He still pitches occasionally for his sons Curt and Donnie's team.

Brothers, teammates, and winners: son Donnie, brother
Charlie, Orville, nephew Wendell, and son Curt

Orville's fast right arm sets the ball in motion
for the Hicks Tree Service Team.

Orville and Charlie sit on the liar's bench at the Aho Recycling Site.
A washtub bass, or gut bucket, stands to to the left.

Orville's pitching hasn't been limited to softball. Years of horseshoe pitching with brothers and cousins sharpened skills that earned him a Watauga County horseshoe pitching championship in 1982.

Orville's experience in the woods is never far from his mind. Alone and with his cousin Ted, Orville watched birds in the woods. He and Ted developed a keen awareness of plant and animal life in the mountains. Orville knows that galax and log moss bring income, oak makes good sled runners, and squirrels make a tasty stew. Despite his knowledge of how to use the natural world, he holds a strong appreciation of the beauty of the woods. He and his brother Jerry have crafted birdhouses from natural materials. Orville used to hunt for food in the woods, but he gave up hunting when he saw that it offended his tenderhearted sons. Now he wins the prize ham or turkey in competitive shooting matches.

Once a boy who spent days among the trees, Orville has chosen to earn his living from outdoor jobs. During their teen years, Orville and Jerry worked with WAMY, a community service agency for Watauga, Avery, Mitchell, and Yancy Counties. The two boys planted trees and shared their earnings with the family. Orville later worked for fifteen years with Hicks Tree Service.

For another fifteen years, Orville has worked for Watauga County as manager of the recycling and container site at Aho. There he enjoys conversation with those who pass. At his work site, Orville built a "liar's bench" from salvaged wood. Folks come by to rest on the rustic bench as they swap yarns. Tour buses have even stopped by the recycling site, just so visitors can meet Orville and hear a quick tale.

Orville says he meets interesting people at work. "A fellow came by in a big white car one day and asked, 'Do you like football?' I said, 'No, sir, but I like softball.' He didn't say no more. Later he came back and asked, 'Do you know who I am?' I said, 'No, sir.' He handed me a fifty-dollar bill and said, 'Go buy yourself a football, son. You might find out that you like it.' I went out and bought myself a softball glove." The fellow in the big car played football with the Miami Dolphins.

"One time a lady from Florida stopped and asked me, 'Are you ashamed of being a mountain man?'" Looking back, Orville can laugh at her insensitive question. How little she knew of Orville Hicks, the gentle, humble storyteller who cherishes his mountain heritage.

Orville, Jr., and his wife, Christie, near the old Stansbury Store

Joe, Wayne, Donnie and Curt

122

Since 1993, Orville and Sylvia have lived near Deep Gap. "It's the foggiest place in the world," says Orville. "It's so foggy you wouldn't believe what I saw coming home the other day. There was a seeing-eye dog trying to help a possum across the road."

All of Orville and Sylvia's sons are grown. Only Joe remains at home. Curt and Donnie live next door in the building that once housed the Stansbury Store and Laxon Post Office. As the family gathers, they reflect on the past: a pet mouse and a sled, apples flung from sticks, memories from Orville's childhood, memories from the childhoods of Orville and Sylvia's sons. Sooner or later, someone mentions Orville's days in the woods. His eyes sparkle.

They recall the lean times—times when they had no electricity, times when Sylvia melted snow for her sons' bath water.

Orville and Sylvia's son Curt sums up his memories. "No matter how hard it was or how low we got on money, Mom and Dad always seemed to get us the things we really needed."

Yet Orville has wanted to give his sons something more important than material goods—something he learned from his own father. "Like Daddy brought us up, I want them to respect everybody and treat everybody like they want to be treated."

A philosophical young man wondered what Orville thought heaven would be like. Orville says, "I told him I think it's going to be about like I growed up."

Orville knows the rewards of having grown up in the mountains. He easily offers a generous list: "Going out in the woods, gathering herbs. Folks from the city don't see all those pretty herbs growing. Hunting. Picking beans, digging potatoes, working eight or nine hours a day when we didn't know how hard we'd worked. Working the mule and the horse, riding on the sled behind 'em. 'Ride us, Daddy! Ride us!' we'd say."

The memories are sweet.

"Life was good," says Orville. "I'd go back if I could."

Narrow, winding NC 194 between Valle Crucis and Matney

RETURN TO THE MOUNTAIN

*The wise ones are the ones who learn
the stories of the people and pass them on.*
—Sharon Kimball

Orville still visits kinfolk around Beech Mountain and Rominger, but twenty years have passed since he walked in the woods of his childhood. On a sunny June day in 2004, he returns to the places of his past.

"I've walked up and down this road many a time," Orville says as he rides up the narrow, winding road above Valle Crucis.

"This is the Big S Curve. Benny and I'd stand at the side of the road and thumb, and then run down the hill and meet the same car when it came around the curve."

Near Rominger Road, he points to a tan brick church. "Mama and Daddy are buried over there. That's not the church where Daddy preached, but a lot of my people are buried there."

At Worley Road, he leaves the car and walks up a path that once was the road to his home. "This was about like a wagon road we used to go down to get to the house."

The old dirt road has been replaced by a tar and gravel road nearby, but the old one holds memories.

"Here's where Daddy built the bus house. We used to climb up that big old tree and get on top of the bus house. And up there's where Russell Farthing kept that bull we had to watch out for." The hillside now grows young Fraser firs for Christmas trees.

"Yonder's the rock where we caught the polecat on the way to school." The overhanging rock forms a shelter almost deep enough to protect a frightened skunk from curious children—almost, but not quite. The pungent skunk scent faded years ago except in Orville's memory.

Teaberry grows abundantly around the rock and through the woods. "You can chew the leaves," says Orville. He picks up a new leaf tip and tastes it, as he did in his childhood.

Orville cuts a six-inch piece of a "laurel," or rhododendron, branch with his pocket knife. He splits one end and slips a laurel leaf into the split, then trims the leaf. "Here's you a crow call." He blows across the split end to make a sound much like the bird's voice. Orville recalls how the children used to make crow calls and blow on them until Mama had her fill of the noise.

Orville picks another leaf, a larger, more tender one this time. He tucks it gently into the circle formed by his thumb and forefinger. A quick slap from the other hand makes a loud pop—homespun entertainment.

Someone has blocked the old road to foot traffic. Deer prints reveal who freely travels the path now. Turning back to the car, Orville takes a short ride to the old home site.

The house that sits in the hollow now is the one built after the homeplace burned. Orville's niece lives there. Only the cellar remains from earlier buildings—now separated from the house by a paved road.

"It's a shame they hard-topped all these backroads," he says.

"I'd come up the old road here and see Mama and Daddy on the porch talking. They'd be grinning to see me coming and know I was okay. They used to worry about us." Orville gazes up the hollow and draws the familiar picture in his mind.

(Clockwise from top) The polecat's hideout; Only the cellar remains; The old dirt road, which led to Orville's home in the hollow, disappears into the woods.

"Sometimes Daddy'd be out on the hill with the mowing scythe. Mama'd be shelling beans on the porch. I wish I could be there now with Mama, shelling beans or bunching galax on the porch."

Orville walks over to the bank near the cellar. "There's one of Mama's huckleberry bushes," he says. White irises bloom around the bush, and grapevines trail across a trellis nearby. Orville's own grin creeps out. "Those huckleberries are so little, it's hard to get a bucketful of them, especially if you eat while you're picking.

"I remember picking strawberries one time, and Mama said, 'You're not eating those strawberries, are you?'" Orville laughs. "I was trying to wipe the juice off my face before Mama saw me."

Orville points downhill from the cellar. "Down there's where we kept the hogs. The boys come out here now and shoot paintballs." Times change.

"It's funny how this all seemed so much bigger when I was a kid," says Orville as he surveys his childhood world.

Orville passes through the site of the old gate where he and Mama encountered a panther long ago, where Mama stood and watched her children walk toward the bus house on school mornings. He walks down the narrow wooded path of the old road and pauses at a worn bridge. "Right here's where I saw the old man go into the woods." A mysterious memory.

Orville pauses by the bridge on the old road. "Right here's where I saw the old man go into the woods."

A familiar creek still washes stones.
"Now, if there was a diamond here, Daddy would have found it."

Walking through woods nearby, Orville pulls up a layer of log moss. "This here's log moss like we used to gather. Sometimes you'd come across a big log, and you could roll off a piece of moss as big as a blanket." He gently sets the moss back on the log. "This will keep growing," he says.

Orville looks at a wash of rocks along the path of a creek. "Now, if there was a diamond here, Daddy would have found it. He was always looking for diamonds. He'd pick up a rock and say, 'I found one! I'm rich!'"

Each turn of the path holds a story. "This rock here's where Boyd and I caught the groundhog. Folks said if you slung a groundhog 'round and 'round a few times, you'd get him dizzy and he wouldn't bite you. Boyd got in front of him, and I got behind him and grabbed him by the hind legs and slung him around." Orville rotates his strong pitching arm to demonstrate. "We got about up to the house, and that groundhog tore into my arm and about tore it off." Orville and his nephew Boyd have some vivid memories of growing up together.

As Orville returns to the paved road near his sister Hattie's home, he finds two young mothers walking with three children. They are kinfolk.

"Hey!" Orville says, his typical cheerful greeting. He pulls out his billfold and offers each child a dollar. He has time to chat with them.

Orville walks across the road to where his brother-in-law Bennie Presnell is working in his yard. Bennie and Hattie's sweet shrub bush blooms by the driveway. "That's a bubby bush like Mama had," says Orville. He picks one of the familiar flowers and rubs the petals to release the sweet scent.

After a neighborly exchange, Orville travels on to Old Mountain Road on Beech Mountain, where Rosa and Ted Hicks still live. Orville visits often, though he sorely misses Ray. Juanita is visiting her mother, and Leonard is spending time there to work on repairs for the aging house which has sheltered four generations of Hickses. Rosa's sons and daughters have helped her plant the big garden that Ray tended for so many years. Flowers around the yard begin their colorful summer bloom.

Orville stops at the spring house to get a sip of cool water with the dipper that hangs by the doorway.

They all sit around the front porch and talk about old times. Ray is part of the conversation, even in his absence. Orville speaks of folks on the mountain— of growing up there.

"The scaredest thing I ever did growing up was hitching that mule. I was afraid he'd kick me. Me and that mule never did get along too well after he bit me." Orville mimics the laughing mule that tormented him as a boy.

Rosa and Orville on the porch

Conversation is peppered with personal stories. Laughter comes easily—from Rosa, from Orville, from Juanita, from Ted. Leonard stops by the porch after unloading a truck full of firewood. He tells about the blizzard of 1960, when a helicopter dropped relief supplies and sent the chickens fluttering every which way from the henhouse.

Orville and Ted speak of fishing, and Orville slips in a short tale of the catfish that followed him home—meowing.

Conversation leads to story, so Orville tells the tale of "Jack and the Devil" and the story of how the man in the moon got there.

131

"Hey, Uncle!" Orville and Ted on the porch

Orville and Ted recall how they used to throw a crowbar to see how far it would go. The idea came from the tale "Jack and the Giant." Orville begins the story. He raises a cupped hand to his mouth and calls out to the giant, as Jack did, "Hey, Uncle!"

An unexpected answer threads its way down the hill from the road, just out of sight. "Hey!" Ted's uncle and aunt had just driven up at a well-timed moment.

Later, Rosa brings out a couple of handmade banjos, each with a local history. Orville and Ted play and sing. Rosa sings "Barbary Allen" as Ted nods appreciation of the familiar ballad.

Around this very porch, folks have shared songs, stories, and conversation since well before Orville's birth. Even without Ray, stories flow forth here as easily as birdsong on a June morning. No one rushes to move on. Everyone has time to talk, to reminisce, to be neighborly.

Orville and Rosa talk about dreams, not wishful dreams, but night dreams that hint of things to come, dreams that warn and prepare. Orville's dreams foretold a death. Juanita tells of once having an unsettling feeling of someone watching her. Soon afterward, an escaped prisoner was captured in the cellar in her yard. Each had sensed a quiet and mysterious voice of divine guidance.

Rosa says she sometimes hears a sound on the porch and momentarily expects Ray to be there. She brings out an album of photographs to show Orville. The album holds pictures of Ray: Ray in his straight chair on the porch, Ray with sons Ted and Leonard, Ray's hands, Ray's funeral, Orville as he sang "The Ballad of Ray Hicks" at the funeral. The last pictures are painful for Orville to see.

Rosa says she once asked Ray, "Why do you talk so much?"

"So I can remember," he said.

Orville laughs and nods. "Yeah." That's why Orville still tells tales—so he can remember.

The hills and hollows are full of stories—Orville's stories. Orville is the keeper of stories, the one who gathers and tells the tales of his people—so we all can know, so we all can remember.

Mountain Wisdom

Orville's family passed along their outlooks on life in words and actions. Orville recalls gems of mountain wisdom that have guided life from childhood to the present.

Respect

Daddy always said to treat other people the way you want to be treated. Have respect for everybody and be good to people.

Mama'd say, "Now, don't you tell somebody to do something you wouldn't do yourself."

Being Yourself

Mama'd say, "Be yourself. Don't get above your raising."

When I'd be telling a story, Ray always said, "Just be yourself. Don't try to be nobody else."

Kindness and Caring

Be kind to your neighbors. We always cared for each other—our neighbors, our friends. We'd be kind to animals. Daddy told us that they don't understand when people mistreat them.

Sharing

We learned to share. We had to share everything. When we milked the cow, we'd give milk and butter to Hassell too.

We just had one bicycle, so we had to share it. Mama'd say, "One of you ride it up the hill and back, and then let the other one ride it up and back." Growing up, we had to learn how to share.

Choosing Friends

Daddy told us, "Don't get with the wrong bunch, but if you do, just turn and walk away from them."

Cooperation

We tried to get along with everybody.

Sometimes I do more listening than talking.

Responsibility

Daddy said, "Do the best you can do.
If you have to go into debt, pay your bills back."

Honesty

Daddy'd say, "Buddy, buddy let me tell you—you go out there and keep a good name," and Mama'd say, "Leave a good name in the world."

If you've done something wrong, own up to it. One lie leads to another. Eventually it will catch up to you.

Neighborliness

Daddy told us, "If your neighbor needs help, help him. If you need help, don't be ashamed to ask him for help."

Money

When we were growing up, we couldn't get too attached to money. What little we had, we couldn't get attached to.

Daddy'd tell us that a good name is worth a million dollars.

Work

Daddy said, "It's good to do a day's work and then sit on the porch and look back over what you've done."

When we used to go out to work for a neighbor, Daddy'd say, "Now you give him a good, honest day's work for a day's pay."

Patience

With eleven kids, Mama and Daddy had to have patience. If we'd done something wrong, they'd get down and talk to us about it.

There's not much patience now. The world's in a rush, rush, rush.

Ray said, "The world's in too big of a hurry, and nobody knows what they've gone to do when they get there."

Friends

Mama said that one friend is worth more than a million dollars.

Forgiveness

Forgiveness is a real good thing. Daddy'd tell us, "Some things are harder to forgive than others, but you've got to forgive; and some are harder to forget than to forgive." The Bible talks about forgiving.
Daddy pretty much went by the Bible.

Mama'd come up and rub your head and forgive you for doing something.

Conversation

I always enjoyed stopping to talk to someone. That was neighborly—stopping to talk to people.

You might say something that would help somebody along the way, and somebody might say something that would help you.

Daddy used to say, "You learn a lot by listening."

People used to have time to stop and talk. Now they barely have time to say "Hello" and go on.

Independence

Daddy said, "You're on your own. Try to stay out of trouble and don't do nobody wrong."

Part IV.
Author's Reflections

Orville is Orville.

He is who he is, no matter if he's at home or in front of the president. He's the same no matter who he's standing in front of.

—Chuck Watkins, director of the Appalachian Cultural Museum

Orville Hicks's world is filled with story, but not with pretense. Orville is an honest man, both in fairness and in candor. What you see is the real Orville. The beard is real. The overalls are daily wear, not performance attire. The colorful mountain speech is his own too, well preserved in the hollows around Beech Mountain.

Orville has no need to change who he is or how he presents himself to fit the circumstance. He delights in his roots—his family, his heritage, his childhood, his sweetheart of more than three decades, and his sons.

Orville Hicks has lived in a world filled with kinfolk. By choice, they have had time for stories, for listening, for conversation. The stories Orville Hicks has gathered—the stories he shares—are a treasure trove of history and mountain tradition.

The materialism that drives so much of modern America has no foothold in Orville Hicks. A man of gentleness and generosity, he has wealth, not the wealth that is counted in dollars, but wealth just the same.

Orville has had a good life, and he knows that.

Card game at Ray's: Orville with Ted, Leonard and Ray Hicks

Part V.

Orville's Family

Father:

Gold Hicks was a farmer and unlicensed Missionary Baptist preacher. He was a descendant of early mountain settlers Cutliff Harman and David Hix.

Mother:

Sarah Harmon Hicks was a descendant of Cutliff Harman and granddaughter of legendary storyteller Council Harmon. She shared numerous stories, rhymes, riddles, and songs with her children.

Brothers and Sisters:

Hassell, the firstborn, lived on the mountain near Orville's family and sometimes provided transportation for them. He made several banjoes, played various instruments, and sang.

Hattie moved to Hickory with her husband, Bennie Presnell. She brought Mary and Jerry to live with her for a while to help them get an education. Hattie and Bennie returned to the mountain in the early 1960s.

Frances and her husband, Junior Presnell, operated dairy farms near Hickory and Claremont. Orville and their son Boyd were buddies, and in summer they often spent time together at each other's homes.

Charlie worked on a dairy farm in Siler City. "You about couldn't buy a job in Watauga County back then," he says. Later, he returned to the mountain near the homeplace.

John worked in Hickory in a furniture factory but moved back to the mountain with his own family. He died at age 56.

Nancy gathered herbs with the younger children. She and her husband, Gary, moved to Hudson, North Carolina, while Orville was still young.

Bobby died in a car accident at age 19.

Willis was still at home during Orville's younger years. He gathered herbs with the younger children and later hunted with Orville. He moved across the county to Meat Camp.

Mary and Jerry were twins and the closest to Orville's age. They were frequent companions in play, herb gathering, and garden work. Mary and her husband, Johnny, lived at nearby Rushy Branch. She died in childbirth at age 23. Jerry remained in the area. An earlier hunting and fishing partner for Orville, Jerry still builds birdhouses with him.

Orville is the youngest and the one who continues the family's storytelling tradition.

Wife:
Sylvia Huffman Hicks came to the mountains from Morganton. She accompanies Orville as he tells tales and manages the business aspects of his storytelling. She and Orville have five sons:
Orville, Jr., Wayne, Donnie, Curt, and Joe.

Others:
Ray Hicks and his wife, Rosa, are both cousins of Orville. Ray was widely known for his storytelling, and Rosa sang with him. Ray's example and encouragement led Orville to public storytelling. Ray and Rosa's son Ted and Orville have been lifelong companions. Ray died in April of 2003.

Adie Harmon, Orville's uncle, operated a store at Matney and provided a storytelling model for Orville. His son Bennie has been a companion of Orville's since childhood.

Council Harmon, Orville's great grandfather, left a legacy of storytelling in the Beech Mountain region.

In Orville's Words

Orville's speech reflects the pronunciations of the Beech Mountain region.

banjer: banjo

dulcymor: dulcimer

holler: a mountain hollow; a dip along a mountain slope and between hills, often along a stream's path

feller: fellow

Plants and animals often have names unique to the region. Some names refer to different species elsewhere.

beadwood: witch hazel (*Hamamelis virginiana*)

bubby bush: sweet shrub, sweet Betsy, or Carolina allspice (*Calycanthus floridus*)

honeysuckle: wild azalea, especially flame azalea (*Rhododendron calendulaceum*)

ivy: mountain laurel (*Kalmia latifolia*)

laurel: rhododendron, especially rosebay rhododendron (*Rhododendron maximum*)

mountain tea: wintergreen or teaberry (*Gaultheria procumbent*)

lizard: salamander

panther: mountain lion or eastern puma. Reports have suggested that the eastern puma was no longer living in the mountains of the area after the early twentieth century; however, mountain residents speak of seeing or hearing the big cats.

Other common words have specific meanings.

cellar: a storage building for food, usually above ground or against a hill. A root cellar is dug into the ground.

roastin'ears: corn on the cob

Regional names refer to familiar animals or items.

diddles: chicks

boomer: a small red squirrel

Susiannah: a butterfly, the Silver-spotted Skipper

hog dollar: silver dollar

The Gold Hicks family c. 1950 (left to right) front: Nancy Hicks and Willis Hicks; 2nd row: Frances Hicks Presnell, Hattie Hicks Presnell, Gold Hicks holding Mary, Sarah Hicks holding Jerry, Hassell Hicks, and Thelma Ramsey Hicks; back: Junior Presnell, Grady Harmon, Charlie Hicks, and John Hicks

Orville on stage with his granddaughter, Jenny Lynn Hicks, daughter of Orville Jr. and Christie Hicks

Awards & Honors

Orville has received a number of awards for his contributions to storytelling and to the preservation of Appalachian cultural heritage.

The Brown Hudson Folklore Award was bestowed by the State of North Carolina on March 22, 1997, in recognition of valuable contributions to the study of North Carolina Folklore and the aims of the Folklore Society.

The Kentucky Colonel Award, presented by the governor of Kentucky, October 19, 1990, is Kentucky's highest award. Kentucky Colonels are selected for their contributions to the community, state, or nation, and are recognized as ambassadors of goodwill and fellowship.

The Paul Green Multi-Media Award was given by the North Carolina Society of Historians on November 6, 1999, for his CD, *Orville Hicks: Mule Egg Seller and Appalachian Story Teller.* The award acknowledges Orville's efforts in preserving North Carolina history.

Orville was nominated for the North Carolina Folk Heritage Award, 2005. (Selection pending)

Orville performed at the 2003 Smithsonian Folk Life Festival in Washington, DC, and at the 2005 governor's inaugural celebration, One North Carolina.

CDs, Tapes, and Books

CD:
Hicks, Orville. *Orville Hicks: Mule Egg Seller and Appalachian Story Teller.* Recordings: Boone, North Carolina: Orville Hicks, 1998. Liner notes: Boone, North Carolina: Thomas McGowan, 1998. CD reissued in 2004 with the addition of "The Ballad of Ray Hicks" and Orville's reflections on Ray Hicks.

Audio Cassette:
Hicks, Orville. *Carryin' On: Jack Tales for Children of all Ages.* Whitesburg, Kentucky: June Appal Recordings, 1990.

Hicks, Orville. Mule Egg Seller and Appalachian Storyteller. Recordings: Boone, North Carolina: Orville Hicks, 1998. Liner notes: Boone, North Carolina: Thomas McGowan, 1998.

Video:
The Jack Tales Festival 2002 (with other storytellers). Blowing Rock, North Carolina: Jack Tales Festival, 2002.

Book:
Isbell, Robert. *The Keepers: Mountain Folk Holding on to Old Ways and Talents.* Winston-Salem, North Carolina: John F. Blair, 1999. A chapter and the cover photo feature Orville Hicks.

Orville has also been featured in numerous magazines and newspapers, including *Our State, North Carolina Folklore Journal, The Watauga Democrat, The Mountain Times*, and *The Blowing Rocket.*

Performance information
For more information about Orville Hicks, visit his website: www.geocities.com/orvillehickssite.

Orville Hicks has performed at schools, universities, churches, libraries, museums, festivals, workshops, conferences, reunions, and birthday parties. To schedule a storytelling performance, contact:

> Orville or Sylvia Hicks
> 142 Brown Farm Road
> Boone, NC 28607
> (828)262-1551

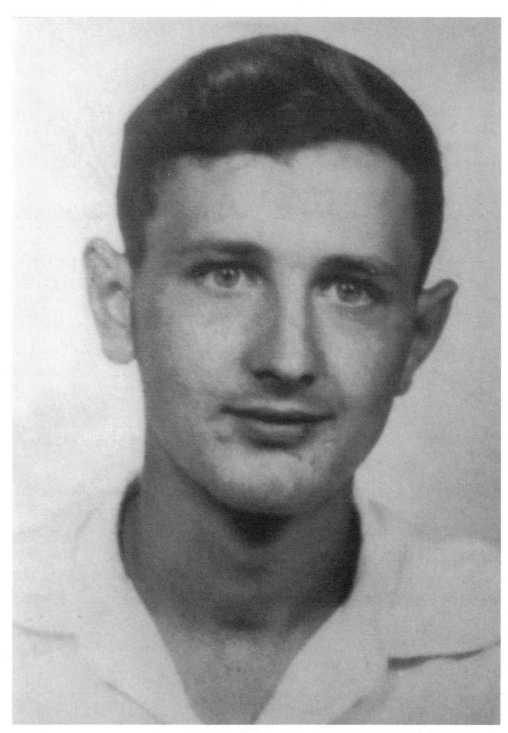

Bobby Hicks, Orville's brother

Acknowledgements

The text of Orville's story comes primarily from conversations I had with him between fall 2003 and fall 2004. His wife, Sylvia, contributed also. I am grateful for their generous support, their gracious hospitality, their patience, and their friendship.

Thanks to Orville's sons, Joe, Curt, Donnie, Wayne, and Orville, Jr., who offered insight, technical support, and encouraging words; to kinfolk across the mountains: to Rosa and Ted Hicks, who welcomed me to their home on Beech Mountain and who shared their wisdom and experience; to Leonard and Juanita, who joined in; to Orville's sister Hattie Presnell and her husband, Bennie, who answered many questions; to sister Frances Presnell and her sons Boyd and David, who happened by at the right time; to brother Charlie and his wife, Alice, both so willing to support the project; to brother Jerry, who helped Orville build a fine birdhouse; to cousin Bennie Harmon, long a companion of Orville's; to the Hicks Tree Service team, who kept winning softball games long enough for me to photograph their part-time pitcher.

Thanks to Alan, my husband, map artist, and technical assistant, who understood the importance of this book, and who traveled with me many times. Thanks to my son John, whose appreciation of the project meant so much; to Joel and Rebecca who heard my questions about digital photography, banjos, butterflies, and more; and special thanks to Joel for tuning the banjo for Ted and Orville on Beech Mountain—by phone from his office in Raleigh.

Thanks to Sharon Kimball and Chuck Watkins of the Appalachian Cultural Museum, who think as highly of Orville as I do.

Thanks to Kenneth Wilcox and Chris Wilcox for broadening my knowledge of the herb business. Thanks also to Tony and Sandy Hayes and Dennis Wood, who helped to educate me about herbs.

Thanks to Pat Koehler, who has believed in me and in Orville's story since I wrote the first words of it, to Carole Weatherford, whose has nurtured me with her experience, and to Trish Perkins and Carole Fox, who have kept me on track.

Thanks to storytellers Dianne Hackworth and Jim Wolfe, to author and illustrator Gail Haley, and to all who graciously contributed photos.

Thanks to my publisher Rao Aluri, who allowed me to stretch my creative vision, and to Aaron Burleson, whose creative expertise brought my vision to the page.

And thanks to Dr. Thomas McGowan, whose own book on Orville I eagerly await.

—*Julia Taylor Ebel*

The best part of writing the book has been meeting two special friends, Julia and Alan.

—*Orville Hicks*

Image & Photo Credits

Front cover photo: Julia Taylor Ebel, photographer

Back cover photos: By permission of Huldah C. Bewley, photographer

Page IV: Julia Taylor Ebel

Page VIII: By permission of Huldah C. Bewley, photographer

Page X: Map drawn by Alan J. Ebel

Page 2: Julia Taylor Ebel

Page 4: By permission of Walter C. Wright, photographer

Page 6, top and bottom: Hattie Hicks Presnell Collection

Page 8, top and bottom: Charlie and Alice Hicks Collection

Page 9: Hattie Hicks Presnell Collection

Page 10: Frances Hicks Presnell Collection

Pages 12; 16; 18, top: Orville Hicks Collection

Page 18, bottom: By permission of Dr. Phillip K Teagarden, photographer; Hattie Hicks
    Presnell Collection

Pages 18, bottom; 19: Hattie Hicks Presnell Collection

Pages 20, 22, 24, 25, 26: Julia Taylor Ebel

Pages 28, 31: Orville Hicks Collection

Page 34, top: Rosa Hicks Collection

Page 34, bottom: Lena McNeely Collection

Pages 37, 38, 40: Julia Taylor Ebel

Page 42: Charlie and Alice Hicks Collection

Page 44: By permission of Claudia B. Hudson, photographer

Page 47: Julia Taylor Ebel

Page 49, top: iStockphotos.com

Pages 49, bottom: 51: Julia Taylor Ebel

Page 52: By permission of Barbara McDermitt, photographer

Page 53, 57: Julia Taylor Ebel

Page 59: By permission of Chris Wilcox

Pages 60, 62, 64: Julia Taylor Ebel

Pages 67; 68, top: Charlie and Alice Hicks Collection

Image & Photo Credits

Pages 68, bottom; 72; 76: Julia Taylor Ebel

Page 78: Frances Hicks Presnell Collection

Pages 79, 82, 84, 85: Julia Taylor Ebel

Pages 86, top and bottom; 88, left and right: Orville Hicks Collection

Page 90: Charlie and Alice Hicks Collection

Page 94: Orville Hicks Collection, Elaine Rines, photographer

Page 95: By permission of *The Watauga Democrat*, Gary Hemsoth, photographer

Page 96: By permission of Joe Young, photographer; Orville Hicks Collection

Page 97: Orville Hicks Collection, photographer unknown

Pages 98, 102: By permission of Joe Young, photographer

Page 103: Orville Hicks Collection

Page 104: By permission of Gail E. Haley, artist

Page 108, all: By permission of Huldah C. Bewley, photographer

Pages 109 and 110: Orville Hicks Collection

Pages 111, 112: Julia Taylor Ebel

Page 114: By permission of Joe Young, photographer; Orville Hicks Collection

Page 116: Julia Taylor Ebel

Page 118: Orville Hicks Collection, photographer unknown

Pages 119, 120: Julia Taylor Ebel

Page 121: Orville Hicks Collection, photographer unknown

Page 122, top and bottom: Orville Hicks Collection

Pages 124; 126, all; 128; 129; 131; 132: Julia Taylor Ebel

Page 140: By permission of Joe Young, photographer

Page 144, top: Charlie & Alice Hicks Collection

Page 144, bottom: Orville Jr. and Christie Hicks Collection

Page 146: Orville Hicks Collection

Page 148: Charlie & Alice Hicks Collection

Efforts have been made to identify photographers. In the event of oversights, corrections will be made in future printings if Parkway Publishers, Inc., is notified.

Julia Taylor Ebel's writings reflect her love of nature and her appreciation of both mountain heritage and family stories. She is the author of **Addie Clawson, Appalachian Mail Carrier**, a biography for all ages and recipient of the Willie Parker Peace History Book Award; and of **Walking Ribbon**, a picture book. Her poems are published in magazines including *Pockets* and *Cricket*. She also tutors and teaches community college classes on children's literature. She lives in Jamestown, North Carolina, but a part of her heart is in the North Carolina mountains, where her hikes lead to poems and conversations lead to stories.